Sports Illustrated

SOCCER

THE SPORTS ILLUSTRATED LIBRARY

BOOKS ON TEAM SPORTS

*Baseball	Football: Defense	Ice Hockey
*Basketball	Football: Offense	Pitching
	Football: Quarterback	*Soccer
		Volleyball

BOOKS ON INDIVIDUAL SPORTS

*Bowling	Skiing	*Women's Gymnastics
*Cross-Country Skiing	Squash	I: The Floor Exercise
Fly Fishing	Table Tennis	Event
*Golf	*Tennis	*Women's Gymnastics
Handball	Track: Running Events	The Vaulting,
Horseback Riding	Track: Field Events	Balance Beam and
Judo	Wrestling	Uneven Parallel Bars
*Racquetball		Events

BOOKS ON WATER SPORTS

*Boardsailing	Skin Diving and Snorkeling
*Canoeing	Small Boat Sailing
Powerboating	Swimming and Diving
*Scuba Diving	

SPECIAL BOOKS

*Backpacking	Safe Driving
Dog Training	Training with Weights

Expanded Format

Sports Illustrated

SOCCER

by DAN HERBST

Photography by
Heinz Kluetmeier

HARPER & ROW PUBLISHERS, New York
Cambridge, Philadelphia, San Francisco
London, Mexico City, São Paulo, Sydney

Thanks for all their help to:

AYSO   Harry Baldwin   Boris Bandov   David Brcic   Mark Bruce   John Carter
Doug Choron   Jeff Durgan   Hilary Engisch   Bob & Janet Ferguson   Lou Gallo
Paul Gardner   Gary Gayle   Skip Gilbert   Stan Green   Brendan Hanley   Ted Howard
Mark Lukas   New York Cosmos   NASL Marketing   Paul Reinhardt   Rye High School Soccer
Program   Jeff Shafranek   Greg Sundberg   University of Vermont Men's & Women's Soccer Pro-
grams   Sasha Von Loewenstein   YMCA Camp Sloane

And an extra special thanks to: Nancy Chaikin   Bill Jaspersohn   Risa Lichter   Alan Mayer
Linda Moran   Mom, Dad, and Diane

American Youth Soccer Organization: pp. 16, 180, 182; John DeFreitas; p. 19 (right); Milton P. Crossen: pp. 38, 67 (left), 130; Gail Megaloudis: p. 61; Stan Green: pp. 64–65 (bottom), 72; Bob Wilson: p. 102; Dan Herbst: pp. 19 (left), 28, 31 (left), 76, 84, 86, 95, 183, 184; courtesy of the Kansas City Comets: p. 14 (right). For *Sports Illustrated*: Jerry Cooke: p. 10; Manny Millan; cover, pp. 11, 27 (left), 31 (right), 113 (right); John McDonough: p. 14 (left); Co Rentmeester: p. 29; Tony Duffy: p. 60; Robert Royal: p. 63; George Tiedemann: p. 105 (right); Andy Hayt: p. 116; George Long: p. 185. All other photographs by Heinz Kluetmeier.

FIRST EDITION

Designer: C. Linda Dingler

Library of Congress Cataloging in Publication Data

Herbst, Dan.
    Sports illustrated soccer.

    1. Soccer. I. Sports illustrated (Time, inc.)
II. Title.
GV943.H375   1983   796.344'2   83–47533
ISBN 0-06-015078-5   85 86 87 88   10 9 8 7 6 5 4 3 2
ISBN 0-06-091083-6 (pbk.)   85 86 87 88   10 9 8 7 6 5 4 3 2

Contents

Preface

For over a century, soccer has been the world's most popular sport. The World Cup Final, held once every four years, attracts a television audience estimated in excess of one billion viewers, and the Federation Internationale de Football Association (FIFA), soccer's international governing body, boasts almost as many member nations as the UN.

Until recently, only North America seemed unaffected by soccer's influence. In 1967 the inevitable happened when soccer and a sports-crazy continent began discovering one another. Previously restricted primarily to ethnic groups in urban enclaves, soccer produced two professional leagues. Before long, the sport's growth attracted people from the entire spectrum of North American society.

Although participation has mushroomed on all levels since, most impressive is its increase among youth. Statistics compiled by the United States Youth Soccer Association (USYSA) illustrate the game's dramatic grass-roots development. In 1975, for example, 103,432 people under nineteen were playing in USYSA-affiliated programs. Three years later, three out of the four USYSA regions registered more participants

9

Size is not a major factor in soccer.

The World Cup Final is the most celebrated sporting event in the world.

apiece than the entire nation had in 1975, and by 1983 over a million athletes were involved. More important, USYSA figures represent only a tip of the North American iceberg since recreation-oriented organizations, such as the YMCA and AYSO (American Youth Soccer Organization), as well as Canadian youth leagues, aren't included in these calculations. A 1982 A. C. Nielsen report, received by the North American Soccer League (NASL), estimated that 7 to 8 million Americans play soccer, of whom nearly half were under the age of twelve.*

Why the incredible growth? The answer is easy.

Soccer is fun.

It's also safe, economical, simple in concept, and healthy. There are no minimum size requirements. The 5'10" athlete, considered small by modern basketball or football standards, would have to glance *downward* to look Pelé in the eye. Too, its boosters consider soccer to be the most "democratic" of all team sports—and they're probably right. There are no written restrictions on a player's movement, no places to hide the less-than-average player, and all players (except the goalie) partake in the joys of offense *and* the responsibilities of defense.

By contrast, in football, almost every child wants to play quarterback. And who wants to play right field in baseball, where action is as rare as steak tartare?

There are no middle guards or right fielders in soccer. Players interchange positions according to the dictates of a game's ebb and flow, with all required to possess (and use) a full range of skills. Each player's role is of comparable importance and all are part of soccer's nonstop action.

Anyone who plays soccer speaks a truly universal language. Put a soccer

*NASL Press Release, November 5, 1982.

ball between children from Nigeria, China, Peru, Iceland, or Egypt and communication results instantaneously.

Such situations occur daily. Numerous tournaments geared for everyone from adults to grammar-school youngsters feature teams from all over the globe. "Recreational" leagues also abound, ensuring that soccer's benefits are never restricted to the gifted few.

Of those in the United States, the AYSO is the most prominent. Based on an "everyone plays" philosophy, AYSO emphasizes fun, exercise, friendship, and cooperation. All participants play at least half of every game, and, although coaches encourage players (male and female) to do their best, the importance of winning is deemphasized.

Not only does soccer offer its participants excellent exercise, it's also among the safest of team sports. The risk of injury is so modest, especially for youngsters, that Dr. Michael Ryan, a Maryland pediatrician and AYSO parent, says, "Kids stand a greater risk of injury going to and from practice or simply by playing in their backyard."

What does one need in order to play the game?

The British answer with an expression: "A boy, a ball, and a wall." Actually, the wall is a luxury. In fact, underprivileged children have even substituted an imaginative array of materials for a ball. All things considered, lack of equipment shouldn't deter anyone from playing this beautiful sport.

Anyone, you say? That's right. The boom isn't limited to kids. Adult leagues for both sexes (as well as co-ed leagues) are cropping up from coast to coast. You are never too old or unskilled to start playing. Many an "old-timer" was introduced to soccer by his children. And fell in love with it on sight.

The fact is, if you take care of yourself and are in good health, you needn't retire from the playing fields at an early age. Former St. Louis University coach Harry Keough has not only fathered a member of the U.S. National Team (Ty Keough) and coached his Bilikens to five NCAA titles, he also still plays several times a week in a co-ed league with his daughter, Peggy, and in St. Louis' Over-30 League, a senior circuit that features more than twenty teams, several

In the city or the country, on pavement or on grass, soccer can be played almost anywhere.

of whose players average age exceeds forty. Now in his late fifties, Harry Keough still looks forward to many more good years of playing soccer.

But older men aren't the only "adult" soccer beneficiaries. The sport has proved to be a most popular activity for women, too. Because soccer emphasizes skill instead of bulk, many females can, and do, compete on an equal footing with men. Former University of Vermont women's soccer team star Hilary Engisch plays in her state's competitive Amateur League. Despite standing but five feet tall, she more than holds her own against her male counterparts.

Hundreds of colleges now field women's varsity soccer teams that vie for a national championship held annually. With each passing season the caliber of play has improved, and now the NASL roster of game officials includes a woman, California's Betty Ellis.

THE INTANGIBLE BENEFITS

Because of its unparalleled internationalism, soccer affords the opportunity to play with and against people from all corners of the globe. As a player, I gained much from this aspect of soccer life. I will never forget, for example, the time my Coe College team hosted Illinois' Palmer College, whose roster was full of foreign-born players. After the game we provided their side with board and room for the night. The player who stayed in my dormitory had escaped from Czechoslovakia under a hail of gunfire. Talking and listening to him, I learned more about priorities, freedom, and just what incredible good fortune I had enjoyed all my life than four years of college could ever have taught.

Later, despite my modest playing skills, I was lucky enough to tour Great Britain with an all-star collegiate squad in 1974. As the personal guests of our rival teams, we got to know our hosts on a one-to-one basis, thus experiencing an England that few tourists ever get to see.

For every soccer player, even those on the youth level, such travel opportunities abound. Ontario's Robbie Cup annually brings together youngsters from four (or more) continents, and one need not be an exceptional player to take part in this or similar events. Furthermore, the work done to raise moneys for such trips reinforces some of soccer's strongest qualities, including working together for a common goal, making individual sacrifices, and striving to realize one's potential.

Dutch superstar Johan Cruyff, considered by many to be the game's greatest midfielder ever, also points out that "soccer teaches you to live with your mistakes, for it is impossible to play the game without making some."

Nevertheless, it is the ability to overcome one's own errors coupled with

soccer's limitless possibilities and endless movement that make it so satisfying
a game to play or watch.

THE PROFESSIONAL AND THE COLLEGE GAME IN AMERICA

With the growth of soccer on these shores has come a commensurate rise in the quality of the professional game here. It's hard to believe, but as recently as two decades ago there was no major-league soccer in North America.

Starting with a combined total of twenty-two teams, the United Soccer Association and the National Professional Soccer League began play in 1967. Buoyed by a wave of optimism, club owners produced seven-figure budgets that begat only four-figure crowds. As a result, within two years only five franchises remained in the North American Soccer League, an amalgamation of the two rival circuits.

For the next five years the NASL managed to survive on shoestring budgets and the dogged determination of a handful of pioneers. Slowly expanding, it developed solid franchises in Vancouver, Seattle, and San Jose. By 1974, fifteen teams formed the NASL. Although it still consisted mostly of semi-professional athletes of modest skills, the league made significant progress.

Then, in 1975, a single act gave U.S. and Canadian soccer a much-needed boost. Gambling an estimated $5 million—roughly equivalent to the entire league's player payroll at that time—the New York Cosmos lured the incomparable Pelé out of retirement. In signing a star of such magnitude (Pelé's desire to visit the troops had brought about a temporary truce in the bitter Biafran Civil War), the Cosmos—and the NASL—were immediately transformed from nonentities into two of the world's most glamorous and famous sporting organizations. A flood of big-name stars soon followed. Within two years Rodney Marsh, George Best, Gordon Banks, Carlos Alberto, Eusebio, Franz Beckenbauer, Bobby Moore, and Giorgio Chinaglia joined the NASL fold. Later arrivals would include Cruyff, Alan Ball, Teofilo "Nene" Cubillas, Jan van Beveren, Karl-Heinz Granitza, Alan Hudson, Gerd Mueller, Ruud Krol, Kevin Hector, Vladislav Bogicevic, Trevor Francis, Brian Kidd, and Duncan McKenzie.

As the quality of play improved, so did attendance. The 1972 average of 5338 spectators per match nearly tripled by 1977—a season capped by an extraordinarily memorable championship contest. An emotional New York squad gave Pelé the perfect retirement "present," edging Seattle 2-1 before a

Soccer's number one goodwill
ambassador, the
incomparable Pelé.

Indoor soccer, as played by the
MISL, has proven to be
extremely popular with North
American fans.

standing-room-only crowd in Portland's Civic Stadium. Of equal significance, the Cosmos' three final home dates attracted sellout crowds to 76,891-seat Giants Stadium.

In 1978, the Major Indoor Soccer League (MISL) opened shop with six clubs. As its name implies, the new kid on soccer's North American block concentrates its energies solely on the six-a-side winterized version of the sport. Played on a hockey rink covered with an artificial turf and with goals built into the endboards, indoor soccer offers fast-paced, high-scoring action.

Operating on more modest budgets than its older counterpart, the MISL grew to fourteen teams by its fifth season. Like the NASL, it has been dominated by its New York franchise, the Arrows. Led by Steve Zungul's scoring feats, the Arrows captured the first four MISL titles with relative ease.

However, not all has been rosy in the professional ranks. Hampered by questionable management decisions and attendance problems in several cities, both leagues have suffered casualties in a number of markets, and network television contracts, save for cable, have eluded both organizations.

Nevertheless, the future of the pro game seems assured because of a factor more significant than the present-day fortunes of the professional game: the mushrooming number of youngsters playing the sport.

The ticket buyers of tomorrow, young players are making their presence felt at every level of the game, and even now that presence is manifest in the current crop of native American pros in the NASL and MISL. Branko Segota, Shep Messing, Rick Davis, Bob Lenarduzzi, Charlie Fajkus, Alan Mayer, Tino Lettieri, Bob Iarusci, Joey Fink, Gerry Gray, Ty Keough, Tony Bellinger, Joe Morrone, Rudy Glenn, Wes McLeod, Mark Peterson, Jack Brand, Steve Pecher, and Bob Rigby have all earned places in pro lineups. Although none of them inspires comparisons with the Pelés or Zunguls, all can certainly be considered solid pros even by demanding European or South American standards.

On campus, the game is growing more popular with each passing autumn. Attracted by soccer's safety and economy, many schools have substituted the international form of football for the domestic variety. In addition, several colleges have built stadiums to house their varsity teams, with soccer now a major draw in places like Duke University, Indiana University, and the University of Connecticut.

As you might guess, this dramatic increase in participation has brought forward a tremendous need for qualified referees and coaches. Scores of people, many of them parents (and nearly all volunteers), can be found in virtually every American community, doing their best to teach a sport that many didn't know existed a few years before. If you are a soccer parent, hello: I know what you're going through, know some of the difficulties you might be having if you're a youth coach, and I've designed this book, in part, as a survival manual to help you and the children you are coaching better understand, and thereby enjoy, the many facets of this sport. I've included drills that will help your team sharpen its skills and teach them to play as a unit, but a word of caution here: go lightly with younger boys and girls; keep the practice sessions simple and unstrenuous; and above all else, keep games and practices what they should be: good, clean fun.

Now for you players out there, whether youth, high-school, college, or adult: This book will lead you through soccer's basic skills—shooting, trapping, passing, dribbling, heading, marking, tackling, and goalkeeping—and show you how to apply those skills in game situations. For any of you to whom the sport's vernacular is a foreign language, I've included a glossary, which begins on page 186.

Even if your involvement in soccer is limited to being a spectator, the fundamentals outlined on the following pages can help you appreciate the subtle beauty of a well-played soccer match. It is to the countless soccer neophytes, both youth and adult, that this work is dedicated.

1

Playing the Game

One reason for soccer's startling growth and popularity is its simplicity. With the notable exception of the offside law, soccer's objective and rules are remarkably easy for the beginner to understand. A team consisting of eleven players tries to advance the ball into its opponent's goal without using hands or arms. The side that scores the most goals wins. The only player who can use his hands is the goalkeeper, and then only within the 44-by-18-yard rectangle in front of his goal known as the *penalty area.*

Limited physical contact with the upper body is permissible so long as the ball is touched first. Other forms of physical contact, such as holding, pushing, charging, and tripping, are fouls. If the ball leaves the field (goes out of bounds), play stops and the team that did not touch it last is awarded possession at the restart.

In general, games consist of two halves, each 45 minutes long, and are presided over by one referee whose judgment is final. He is assisted by two linesmen.*

Field dimensions vary, although 110 by 70

*At collegiate and scholastic levels, games are sometimes handled by two officials of equal authority. Games may also be shorter and can be divided into quarters.

17

Two of the American Youth Soccer Organization's 250,000-plus participants.

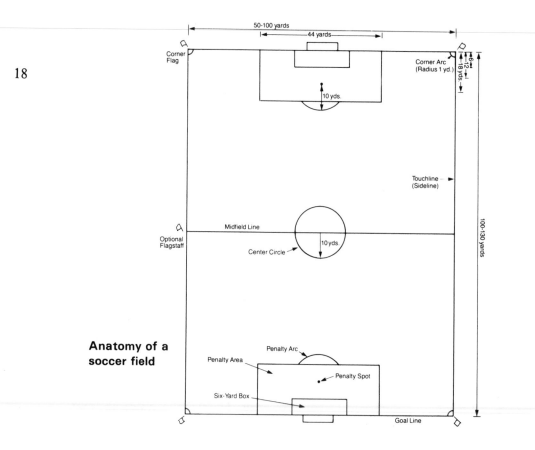

Anatomy of a soccer field

50-100 yards

44 yards

Corner Flag

Corner Arc (Radius 1 yd.)

10 yds.

Touchline (Sideline)

6 — 12 — 18 yds.

100-130 yards

Midfield Line

Optional Flagstaff

10 yds.

Center Circle

Penalty Arc

Penalty Area

Penalty Spot

Six-Yard Box

Goal Line

yards is a fairly common size. Dimensions can legally range from 100 to 130 yards in length and 50 to 100 yards in width. Centered at each end are the goals, measuring 24 feet wide and 8 feet high.

Although a coach can allocate his players as he sees fit, all formations consist of forwards, midfielders, defenders, and a goalkeeper. Their roles and responsibilities vary, but soccer's freeflowing nature allows its participants to become involved in virtually all phases of the game. This lack of regimentation —individual freedom, if you will—is one reason soccer has been called the most democratic of all team sports. Each player must possess a wide range of skills coupled with dexterity and the ability both to anticipate situations and react to them with the appropriate response.

No matter what your station, knowing the laws of the game is a must.

FREE KICKS

In soccer, fouls are penalized by awarding either a direct or indirect free kick. The ball is placed at the spot of the infraction, with all members of the offending team required to retire at least 10 yards from it until the ball is put into play.

If a defender infringes upon this neutral zone, the kick may be retaken at the referee's discretion.

A *direct free kick* results when one of soccer's "major" fouls—i.e., kicking, pushing, tripping, holding, striking, or jumping at an opponent, charging violently or from the rear, or handling the ball—is committed. A *hand ball* is defined as intentionally touching the ball with an arm or a hand by any player except the goalkeeper when within his own penalty area.

On a direct kick, the ball may be shot into the goal without touching another player.

Less serious infractions are punished by an *indirect free kick*. On an indirect kick, the ball must touch at least two players before a goal can be scored. Examples of indirect free kick offenses include a *dangerous play* (whereby a person's actions jeopardize his own or another player's safety *even though no contact occurs*) and *obstruction* (illegally using one's body to impede an opponent from playing the ball).

An indirect free kick will also be awarded against a team for charging an opponent when the ball is not within playing range, charging the goalkeeper within the penalty area, or when a goalkeeper takes more than four steps when in possession of the ball.

Fouls that are either vicious or intentionally employed to gain a tactical advantage (a defender who is out of position might catch the ball as it flies over his head), fighting, ungentlemanly conduct, or excess dissent with the officials can be further punished. The referee may caution or eject the player and signal the decision by holding aloft a yellow or a red card. The *yellow card* is an official

Even though the player on the left *tried* to play the ball, he is guilty of tripping since he made contact with his opponent's body instead.

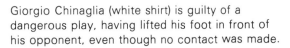

Giorgio Chinaglia (white shirt) is guilty of a dangerous play, having lifted his foot in front of his opponent, even though no contact was made.

warning, serving notice that any further misconduct will result in that player being ejected from the contest, with his team forced to play the remainder of the match shorthanded. A *red card* signifies instant removal. The issuance of a second yellow is equivalent to the red.

This system contrasts with the old method of "booking" players. Prior to the 1970 World Cup, the referee wrote an offending person's name in a notebook while orally warning the athlete. Due to soccer's internationalism, communication was often impossible. Many times ejected players would claim they had no knowledge of the initial booking, and spectators and coaches were also often unaware of these warnings. So this system was aided by adding the use of yellow and red cards.

THE ADVANTAGE LAW

Soccer may be the only sport in which there are instances where a foul is intentionally ignored. When whistling an infraction against the defending team would prove disadvantageous to the attackers, the referee allows the game to "play on."

Let's say, for example, the New York Cosmos are facing the Vancouver Whitecaps. Rick Davis has dribbled past several opponents and is advancing toward the Vancouver goal when Whitecap defender Bob Lenarduzzi trips him. Although Davis stumbles, he regains his balance and maintains possession as he gets by Lenarduzzi. To halt play at this point would aid Vancouver, negating a better scoring opportunity than would be presented by a free kick from the point of the foul. Thus, the advantage law goes into effect and play is not interrupted. Should the referee wish, he can still caution or eject the fouling player during the next stoppage of play.

THE PENALTY KICK

When a direct-kick offense—kicking, pushing, tripping, etc.—is committed by the defending team within its own penalty area, soccer's most severe punishment is employed. Known as the penalty kick, it almost always results in a score.

The ball is placed 12 yards in front of the center of the goal. The goalkeeper must stand on the goal line and cannot move his feet until the ball has been kicked. All players, except the shooter and the goalie, must vacate the penalty area and be at least 10 yards from the ball until the shot is taken. It is virtually impossible for a keeper to thwart a properly taken penalty without cheating (i.e., moving his feet before the ball has been kicked).

Direct, indirect, and penalty kicks are but three forms of restarts. Any time the *entire* ball crosses the *entire* out-of-bounds line, play is temporarily halted. If the ball has crossed the sideline (or, in soccer terminology, gone "into touch"), play is resumed with a *throw-in,* which is taken from the spot where the ball crossed the line.

The thrower must stand outside the field. He puts the ball back into play by tossing it over his head with both hands. Both feet must remain on the ground and the player must throw the ball in the direction that he is facing. If the thrower violates any of these regulations, the opposing team is awarded a throw-in. Until the ball has been touched by another player, the thrower is ineligible to touch it a second time. Just as with an indirect free kick, a goal will not be awarded should the ball be thrown into the net without first touching another player.

A different restart method is used whenever the ball crosses the goal line without entering the goal. If the defending team last touched the ball, the attacking team is awarded a *corner kick.* The ball is placed within a yard from where the sideline and goal line intersect at the corner nearest the spot where the ball left the playing field. All defenders must stand at least 10 yards from the ball until it is kicked. Just as with a direct free kick, a goal can be scored without a second player touching the ball.

If the attacking team last touched the ball before it crossed the goal line, a *goal kick* results. The ball is placed within the 6-yard box in front of the defending team's net to the side of the goal closer to where the ball left the field. Any member of the defending team can put the ball back into play. The ball may not be touched by another player until it has fully left the penalty area. Failure to comply with any of these stipulations results in the goal kick being retaken.

Play can also be restarted with a *drop ball.* This occurs when two opposing players are equally guilty of fouling, when play has been halted to attend to an injury, or when the official is unsure who last touched the ball before it went out of bounds.

On a drop ball, a player from each team faces his opponents' goal. The referee drops the ball, which may be played by either of the two rivals as soon as it strikes the ground.

A game (and all subsequent periods) is begun with a *kickoff.* The ball is placed at the center of the midfield line. Play starts with a free kick in which all of the defending team's players must be at least 10 yards from the ball and on their team's side of the midfield line until it is kicked. The player taking the kickoff must propel the ball at least one full revolution forward and cannot touch it again until it has been played by at least one other person.

Teams alternate initiating kickoffs as each new period begins. Kickoffs also occur following a score, with the team that gave up the goal awarded possession —that is, the right to kick off.

OFFSIDE LAW

As noted, soccer's rules and regulations are simple with one major exception: the offside law. Instituted to prevent "basket hanging," it causes as much controversy in a match as all other rules combined.

Stated in its simplest form, the law says that a player is offside when he does not have at least two defensive players between him and the defending team's goal line when the ball is played forward by a fellow attacking player.

There are a number of modifications to the law. A player cannot be offside if he receives the ball directly from a corner kick, throw-in, or an opposing player. Technically, he is only offside if he is judged to have *gained an advantage* by being in such a position (a clause whose interpretation is constantly debated). A player cannot be offside if he is on his team's side of the midfield line when the ball is played forward, or if he is behind the ball.

The key point is that a player's positioning is *only relevant at the instant the ball is played forward.*

Offside and onside. In diagram A, X1 passes to X2, who is *onside* because O3 and the goalkeeper (GK) are between him and the goal line as the ball is played forward.

In diagram B, X1 passes to X2, who is *offside* because he has only one player (the goalkeeper) between himself and the goal line as the ball is played forward.

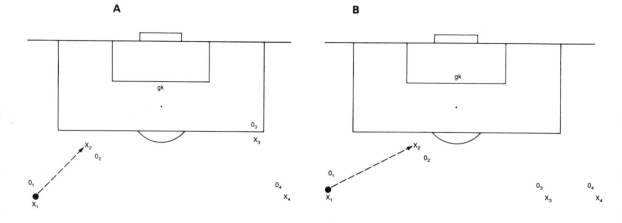

SUBSTITUTIONS

Until relatively recently in its history, soccer was literally an eleven-player game. The first World Cup substitute did not appear until the 1970 tournament. Prior to that, injured athletes faced an option: persevere or leave their teammates to carry on a player short.

Gradually, the laws were modified and FIFA now permits a maximum of two changes per professional match. Some outposts of conservatism (notably England, where the game is said to have originated) allow but one substitute. Furthermore, in the English League, the twelfth player must be designated prior to the opening kickoff. Usually, that man is a versatile athlete. Indeed, English football is ripe with stories of outfield players having to test their skill in goal after the starting keeper was sidelined with an injury.

Not surprisingly, English managers are reluctant to use their substitution, particularly during the early stages of a match. Should a player be temporarily rendered out of commission, he will often retire to the sideline for repairs while his team continues with ten players. At a stoppage of play (and with the referee's official permission), he can return to action so long as no substitution has been made.

The youth, scholastic, and collegiate rules in North America are extremely generous. Not only are there no limitations on the amount of substitutions, but players are also permitted back into a match after being removed. This modification of soccer's international rules has generated great criticism from many students of the game who feel that it allows players to avoid pacing themselves. These critics claim that what all too often results is a helter-skelter version of the sport in which sprinting ability is more important than skill.

There are certain restrictions as to when a substitution can be made. In professional soccer, a change is permitted during any stoppage of play and with the referee's permission. College rules allow player changes when the ball has crossed the goal line (including after the scoring of a goal) and when an injury occurs. In the latter situation, only the injured player may be removed, with the opposition also allowed one change. The same holds true in some leagues after a caution has been issued: the coach may substitute a player for the offender, with the other team also allowed one switch.

Many youth and scholastic leagues permit substitutions when the ball crosses the goal line, when there is an injury or a card, after a score, and when the team making the move(s) has a throw-in. At these levels, rules and regulations vary considerably.

The one position in which substitutions are rare is in goal. When a change in keepers is made, the new goalie must report to the referee.

LENGTH OF GAMES

Although a soccer match is generally thought of as a 90-minute affair, there can be plenty of variance. Rule 7 states that matches "shall be two equal periods of 45 minutes unless otherwise agreed upon." In some leagues, the NASL among them, overtime is employed whenever a tie exists after regulation time. U.S. collegiate play calls for 20 extra minutes of non-sudden-death action. At most other levels, matches that are drawn after 90 minutes remain so unless they are championship contests, in which case a 30-minute, non-sudden-death overtime is added.

The official time is kept by the referee. The clock stops when a serious injury needs attention on the field, when one team is judged to be wasting time in restarting play, or when the ball is temporarily lost after leaving the playing surface. This is all refered to as "injury time" and is added to the end of the period.

Many leagues play shorter games. The younger the players, the less time a match should last. The USYSA recommends the following times for youth contests:

AGE	TIME
Under-8	50 minutes (two 5-minute overtimes)
Under-10	50 minutes (two 10-minute overtimes)
Under-12	60 minutes (two 10-minute overtimes)
Under-14	70 minutes (two 10-minute overtimes)
Under-16	80 minutes (two 15-minute overtimes)
Under-19	90 minutes (two 15-minute overtimes)

The Canadian Soccer Association further suggests that all Under-10 play involve seven players per team and be contested on a 60-by-50-yard field with goal size scaled down proportionately. Like their U.S. counterparts, the CSA calls for shorter games for younger players.

TIE-BREAKING

Overtimes aren't the only ways of eliminating draws. In championship international games that are tied after extra time, one of two options is used. Either the entire contest is replayed at a later date or kicks from the penalty spot are employed. When the latter is stipulated, each team takes five alternating shots. Just as with penalty kicks, the goalie may not move until the ball is kicked.

Whoever converts more kicks wins the game. Should an equal number be scored by each side, an extra shot per club is taken until one team scores and the other doesn't. No player may attempt a second shot until all of his teammates who were playing at the final whistle have shot once.

In 1976, an interesting tie-breaking method was introduced by the NASL, which noted that penalty kicks inherently produce controversy over whether the keepers had moved too soon. In addition, the penalty-kick tie-breaker meant that games were decided by a shooter's error instead of by a positive play. The new league's answer was called the *shootout.*

In a shootout, the ball is placed 35 yards from the goal, with the keeper starting on his line. Over a 5-second period the attacker may attempt one shot. Neither his nor the goalie's movements are restricted in any way. Just as with penalty-kick tie-breakers, five alternating attempts are mandated, with the same procedure used should the score remain tied after five rounds.

Scholastic soccer tends to utilize unlimited sudden-death overtimes in championship games. Because of its liberal substitution laws, such an approach does not present the significant injury risk that it would if used in a professional match.

OFFICIATING

Soccer matches are presided over by a referee. He is assisted by two linesmen who are strictly advisers.

As the name implies, each linesman is responsible for one sideline and one goal line. Any time a ball crosses an out-of-bounds line under his jurisdiction he points his flag toward the goal of the team that last touched the ball. This is done to indicate to the referee which team he thinks should be awarded possession. Each linesman is assigned half the field of play. He positions himself in a line with the player on the defending team who is the second closest to his own goal line so as to best be able to detect an offside violation. In addition, he will raise his flag whenever he sees a foul in his zone for which the referee was unsighted. *In all cases it is the referee's role to decide whether or not to heed a linesman's advice.* Unlike the referee, a linesman rarely watches the action around the ball. He serves as an extra set of eyes, keeping close tabs to be sure that no illegal activities occur away from the play.

The referee's job demands not only a flawless knowledge of the laws of the game, coupled with sound judgment and an ability to handle people in stressful situations, but also a high degree of physical fitness. He must keep up with the play, a particularly tough chore when the ball is booted 50 yards upfield.

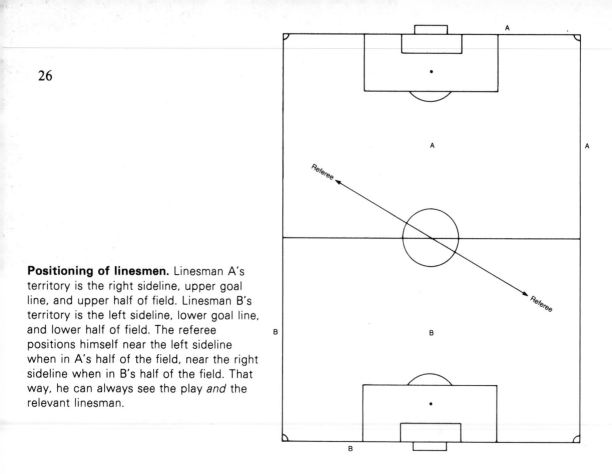

Positioning of linesmen. Linesman A's territory is the right sideline, upper goal line, and upper half of field. Linesman B's territory is the left sideline, lower goal line, and lower half of field. The referee positions himself near the left sideline when in A's half of the field, near the right sideline when in B's half of the field. That way, he can always see the play *and* the relevant linesman.

Positioning is as important to officials as it is to players. If you are called on to referee a soccer match, you should station yourself so that both the play and the relevant linesman are within your view. With rare exception, you'll want to be *behind the ball* (so if it is kicked upfield you can get back in position quickly) and *within 20 yards of the action.* Incidentally, the ref is considered a part of the field, so be warned: Any ball striking you is in play just as if it had hit a goalpost.

POSITIONS

A team consists of eleven individuals who must work together with complimentary abilities. While each position accentuates a specific skill (or skills), all players must possess all-around ability. Because soccer is a free-flowing game, there will be numerous occasions in which defenders will be on the attack and forwards will be defending. Nevertheless, each position does have specific responsibilities and demands different primary assets from a player.

As the last line of defense, the goalkeeper is the only player permitted to touch the ball with his hands or his arms. To help make saves, some goalies wear goalkeepers' gloves, which come in several models.

The Goalkeeper

The main chore of the goalie—the only player permitted to use his hands or arms—is to prevent the opposition from scoring. The keeper must wear a distinctively-colored shirt, one that is different from those worn by either team or by the officials. Many goalies include in their wardrobe padded shorts, long-sleeved shirts (with extra protection over the elbows), shin pads, and special gloves. Although wearing gloves is strictly a matter of personal preference, they are helpful on damp days when the ball is wet and slippery.

Should you decide to play in goal, you will need good hand–eye coordination and quickness. You must be a defensive leader and a player whose abilities, judgment, and courage inspire confidence among your teammates. As a goalie, you are the only athlete who can see the entire field of play, so as an ideal keeper you should continually provide your mates with advice.

Although your position makes you "the last line of defense," you can also initiate counterattacks by making good outlet passes as soon as you've gained possession of the ball.

Forwards

As a forward, you will be concerned primarily with scoring goals. Your ability to create and convert opportunities will often decide a match's outcome. You must be able to shoot powerfully and accurately with either foot and on a split-second's notice. Equally essential is the skill to dribble around an opponent in tight quarters. The outstanding forward makes things happen in the

A forward's chief responsibility is to score goals.

area of the field in front of the opponents' goal, where time and space are at a premium.

To be a successful forward you'll need a high degree of soccer intelligence. Your uncanny knack for being in the right place at the right time is no accident. The truly first-class forward's ability to think and analyze creates as many scoring chances as do his physical skills. Basically, there are two types of forwards.

The Striker

On every team there are one or two central attackers whose job it is to put the ball in the net. They patrol the area in front of the opponents' goal and, like cobras, seize any half-chance with a deadly instantaneous response.

As a striker, you'll need all the attributes listed above as well as unquestioned courage. You must have the guts to place your head where others would not dare put their feet! You must never allow the physical intimidation of defenders to dissuade or distract you. Your concentration should be totally on scoring.

Strikers can also serve as "target" players. As a striker you will often play with your back to the opponents' goal so that you may face your teammates and the oncoming ball. When this occurs, your team may wish to pass you the ball. Unless you are confident you can get open for a shot, you should "hold" the ball until help arrives. At that point, make a pass to a teammate who is running into a good attacking position.

The Winger

Often the quickest player (or players) on the team, the winger has as his domain the area just inside the touchline (sideline). It is his duty to provide service to the striker. To become a classic winger you must be a player who can dribble around opponents at full speed. One-on-one confrontations are your forte. Your ability to beat the widest defender is cherished. When you do this, you force central defenders to vacate the middle of the penalty area, thus creating a chance to cross the ball into the danger zone, which is defensively depleted.

Although most wingers create far more scoring chances than they convert, they must still be able to shoot with either foot. It is equally important that, as a winger, you be able to perform all these tasks while your eyes scan the field. With good vision, you will see teammates moving to open spaces and will be better able to deliver a well-timed and accurate pass.

The Midfielders

Often referred to as a team's "engine room," the midfield unit is charged with a number of important tasks.

Highly energetic and skillful performers, midfielders are also called "linkmen" because they provide a bridge between their team's defenders and forwards. Their control over the central portion of the field can dictate a game's ebb and flow, allowing their team to enjoy a disproportionate territorial advantage.

As a midfielder, you must be able to pass, dribble, and shoot while on offense and support, mark (guard), and tackle on defense. (By "tackling," I don't mean the NFL variety, rather the ability to use your feet to remove the ball from an opponent.)

Your passing sets the tone and pace of the attack. Your ball skills must be refined since loss of possession in the midfield can leave your side extremely vulnerable. You must be an intelligent player, able not only to recognize whether to pass, dribble, or shoot, but who or where to dribble or pass to.

Dribbling is the art of advancing the ball by using one's feet, and midfielders and wingers should be exceptional dribblers.

Midfielders used to be called "halfbacks," and there are several different breeds.

The Attacking Midfielder

Also known as the "maestro," the attacking midfielder is an offensive-minded player. Positioned just behind the forward line, he creates havoc in an opposing defense with his wide range of offensive skills. Featured in his arsenal is the ability to make the "killer pass" that sets up a teammate for a great scoring opportunity, to dribble by defenders, and to shoot with lethal accuracy and power from long range.

A good reader of the game, he is often given license to neglect his defensive duties when an opposition attack does not present a significant danger. He is generally the first man his teammates want to pass to when they regain possession. Many times, when his team is defending, he can be found about 10 to 15 yards upfield and at a slight angle to the ball.

As an attacking midfielder, you'll need excellent control in tight spaces. As the "brains" of your team, you must combine physical and mental excellence with an unselfish nature.

The Defensive Midfielder

In every successful midfield there is always at least one unheralded workhorse whose willingness to perform unglamorous functions allows his mates to take offensive liberties. Also known as the "midfield anchor" or the "ball winner," he varies his role depending on the other team's capabilities and tactics. When playing against a side that features an individual midfield star, the defensive midfielder may be charged solely with marking that player. When facing opponents with a more balanced midfield attack, he reads the situation and positions himself either to thwart the player or guard the zone that presents the greatest potential danger at the moment.

Although defense will be your main concern as a defensive midfielder, you cannot be lacking in offensive skills. The instant that you win possession, a great opportunity is presented. As often as not, many opposing players are left stranded in attacking positions. The time it takes them to make the transition to defense can be used to launch a counterattack. If you can play a skillful, penetrating pass, you can put several opponents "out of the game" on that play, leaving the opposing defense undermanned.

The Two-Way Midfielder

The classic linkman, he can be seen racing full speed to join in on offense or

No matter what position you play, you must be able to use all allowable parts of your body—even your head—to control the ball.

get back on defense. His high work rate and energetic style are important factors in ensuring that his team has numerical superiority as often as possible.* As a two-way midfielder, your repertoire of skills must be balanced. You must be able to pass as well as you tackle and to dribble as well as you mark. On offense, as a two-way midfielder you'll find yourself running to get into dangerous positions, whereupon a teammate can pass you the ball. Defensively, you must be able to ascertain immediately what areas are covered by the backline and the midfield anchor. You must then proceed to the next most dangerous spot or help the defensive midfielder if need be.

Midfield Overview

Under ideal circumstances, all of a team's midfielders are capable of functioning in any of these roles and can interchange at any time depending on the circumstances of the match. For example, if an attacking opportunity presents itself to the defensive midfielder, he should have the inclination and skill to capitalize on it while a teammate temporarily assumes his role and provides defensive cover (i.e., stays *behind* the play so that he will be in good defensive position should his team lose possession).

No matter what level of soccer you play, you should try to develop all-around soccer skills. And you coaches out there should avoid defining midfield roles when dealing with the younger athlete.

A final note on midfield play: On most teams, three or four players are

---

*Numerical superiority is determined by the number of offensive players in attacking positions versus defenders behind the ball.

assigned to the midfield. When a team uses a formation calling for fewer than three midfielders, the role of each player is less well defined.

Defenders

As their name implies, these players are concerned with preventing the opposition from creating scoring opportunities. As a defender, you must be agile enough not to be beaten by the winger and strong enough to win balls in the air. Tackling ability is crucial. So is knowing when to challenge for the ball and when to try merely to slow down the opponents' attack until help arrives.

In modern soccer most teams use four backs. The most common deployment involves three defenders who are each assigned to mark a specific player while the fourth man roams to provide assistance whenever and wherever danger arises. However, some teams prefer to use a zone system in which defenders are responsible for securing a designated territory.

The Fullbacks

In both zone and man-to-man play, the two outside defenders are commonly called fullbacks. It is their job to mark the winger, trying to keep him as wide as possible. Should the other team be playing with only two forwards, one of the fullbacks is concerned with closing down the first midfielder who comes through unmarked. In addition, the fullback can become offensively involved by "overlapping," a term that refers to the situation in which a defender takes the ball and advances offensively ahead of one or more of his team's midfield players. This occurs when he sees that the sideline in front of him is clear and dribbles past the midfield area. When this happens, a midfielder or a forward rotates to take his place defensively.

The Central Defenders

When playing a zone, two central defenders are employed. They work in concert to pick up any attackers who have penetrated unmarked into dangerous positions. As a rule, if you are a central defender, you should be physically robust, a crunching tackler, and strong in the air.

The Stopper

Teams not using a central zone will line up with a stopper and a sweeper. The former is assigned the chore of marking the opposing team's most dangerous attacker, usually the striker. Because the top-quality striker is as smart as he is skillful, if you decide to become a stopper you will need exceptional concentration and judgment. You must never allow your attention to drift nor be suckered into either attempting a tackle at the wrong time or being drawn out of position by your rival's clever off-the-ball running.

You must always be wary of such movements, especially when the play is near a sideline and watching both the ball and your man is difficult. To "ball watch" at such times is to invite disaster, allowing the striker to make an undetected run to get open in front of the goal.

As a stopper, you must be adaptable. You need the quickness to mark the striker who himself relies on quickness (Pelé is a case in point), as well as the strength and courage to thwart the powerfully built forward who is deadly in the air (like 1980 NASL Most Valuable Player Roger Davies).

The Sweeper

Soccer's answer to football's free safety, the sweeper usually plays behind his three defensive mates, constantly analyzing so he can anticipate dangerous situations and react to them before they become crises. Often a veteran player, he is treasured for his mental capacities. As a rule, he tries to stay between the ball and his goal. This position, introduced by the Italians, is also called "libero" (literally "free one"). Until the late 1960s, the sweeper was strictly a defensive player. The great West German star Franz Beckenbauer revolutionized the position by adding offensive responsibilities. Because as a sweeper you can see so much of the field, you must be able to recognize the space created by opponents who are attacking, and, as your team wins the ball, move to exploit that space. Beckenbauer's penchant for leading and joining in on Bayern Munich's counterattacks helped earn him two European Footballer of the Year awards while giving the sweeper's role an extra dimension.

FORMATIONS

Throughout soccer circles there is much talk of "tactics," with, more often than not, the topic of formations at the forefront. Despite the prevalence of such discussions, there really isn't much variation in how coaches employ their players.

With rare exception, all teams (from youth soccer to the pros) feature a goalkeeper and at least three defenders, two midfielders, and two forwards. A coach is left to decide how to use the remaining three players.

The most commonly used formation calls for four defenders, three midfielders, and three forwards (the 4-3-3). Other popular configurations include the 4-4-2 (using twin strikers, with the outside midfielders often acting like

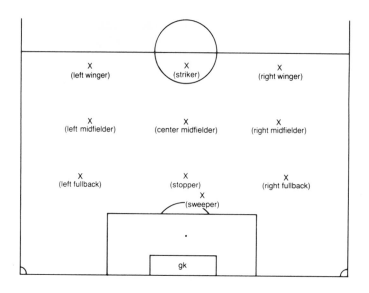

The most commonly used formation in soccer is the 4-3-3.

wingers on offense) and the 4-2-4. At youth levels, or when you're facing a team using fewer than three forwards, the 3-4-3 and 3-3-4 become viable alternatives.

If you're a coach, the key factor is not how *many* players you commit to offensive positions but *how* you instruct them to play. A 4-4-2 *can be* an attack-minded formation *if* the midfielders are encouraged to go forward. A 4-2-4 *can be* defensive *if* your team uses a lot of safe passes and aims to play a possession style of game with an emphasis on getting nearly all of your players behind the ball on defense.

All of which is a far cry from the early days of soccer, when roles were strictly defined and two players on defense was the norm. As recently as three decades ago, defenders defended, halfbacks played both ways, and forwards attacked. As soccer evolved it became more defensive. The offside law was modified in 1925 so that an attacker needed two, instead of three, defensive players between himself and the goal line when the ball was played forward.

During the 1950s, the so-called "W-M" became *the* formation. Using five forwards, it got its name from the way the players lined up. If one drew a line between the forwards and another line from the halfbacks to the defenders, the letters *W* and *M* were formed (see diagram). By the sixties, the W-M's defensive

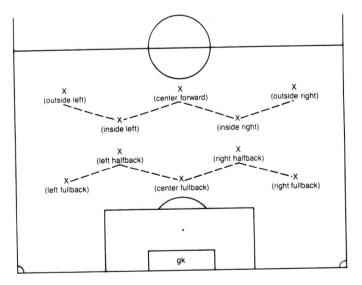

The W-M formation derives its name from the two letters "spelled out" by the forwards, and by the halfbacks and the defensemen.

shortcomings (with too few players defending, a lot of goals were given up) were becoming increasingly apparent. A fourth defender was added to most teams' alignments, thus doubling the pre-1925 quotient.

The Italians soon introduced "catenaccio" to the sport's vocabulary, a system that stood for more defensive rather than offensive players, including a libero, and significantly fewer goals.

Fortunately, from a fan's viewpoint, the offensive brilliance and international success of the Pelé–led Brazilians captured three of four World Cups beginning in 1958. Their influence is still felt today.

In the 1974 World Cup, an approach was introduced by Coach Rinus Michels' Netherlands team. Nicknamed "the Clockwork Orange" for their marvelous efficiency and teamwork, the Dutch originated the concept of "total soccer." Under Michels' scheme, all players were expected to attack when their team had the ball and all defend when without it. The forward and defensive lines were separated by far less space than had been the norm in the past, making Holland's transitional game lightning-quick.

The only drawback was the need for a roster full of highly skilled players in peak physical condition coupled with a level of understanding that can only be realized through extensive play together. Thus, Michels' brainchild does not work as well for U.S. or Canadian high-school teams, say, as it does at the professional level.

Nevertheless, its priorities can be universally adopted. Because soccer is such a fluid and unrestricted game, it is highly unlikely that all—or even most—scoring opportunities will present themselves to the striker. It is equally probable that, several times during a game, a team's nondefenders will be called upon to thwart a dangerous scoring threat. In "total soccer," *all* players must achieve a minimum degree of competence in *all* facets of the sport. So while "total soccer" as illustrated by the Dutch teams of the 1974 and 1978 World Cups may not be applicable to youth soccer, the need to develop all-around skills in all players applies. If you coach a youth team, I strongly urge that you *make each player play every position,* regardless of a boy's or girl's talent. And if you're a youth player, learn the *whole game,* not just the skills applicable to your favorite position. Think of it this way: As a person and player, you're still growing; your value at any one position may change. A player who can play any position is extremely valuable to his team. Furthermore, every time you perform in a new role, you will hone the skills that position accentuates and you will gain a better understanding of the overall game. Doing so will help make you a "complete player."

EQUIPMENT

One of the beauties of soccer is that you need so little equipment to play it. A pair of sneakers and a ball can suffice. Even on an organized level, it often costs less to outfit an entire soccer *team* than to equip one ice-hockey or football *player!*

The only indispensable piece of equipment is the ball. A regulation-size ball is 27 to 28 inches in circumference and weighs 14 to 16 ounces. Because young players may experience difficulty kicking a ball designed for adult use, smaller balls are manufactured for youth teams. The USYSA recommends a size-3 ball (23 to 24 inches in circumference) for players under eight years old and a size-4 (25 to 26 inches) up to age twelve.

Soccer uniforms tend to be simple and economical. They consist of a shirt, shorts, socks, and shoes, and may be augmented by the use of shin guards. In fact, I strongly recommend wearing shin guards, and to male players I further recommend an athletic supporter. The uniform should fit comfortably, allowing

Soccer balls come in three basic sizes, the smaller models being for youth and junior players. Soccer shoes come in a wide variety of cleat configurations, including ripple-soled models for play on artificial surfaces.

freedom of movement, and should be made of a light material unless specifically designed for use in a cold climate.

The quality of shoe (or boot) varies considerably. For the novice, a modestly priced shoe should suffice, but don't sacrifice comfort for price. Most shoes come with cleats, and there are as many cleat configurations as there are manufacturers making them. Ripple bottoms are also available, for use on artificial surfaces such as Astroturf. Take care of your shoes. Along with your body, they're your most important piece of equipment. If you get your shoes wet, stuff them with newspaper so they don't lose their shape, and polish them regularly to protect the leather. Remember: Shoes that are neglected will wear out prematurely, losing much of their flexibility and comfort.

As mentioned earlier, goalkeepers require special equipment, but the same safety and comfort considerations should prevail.

Field equipment includes two goals with nets, four corner flags (to indicate where the sideline and goal line intersect), and a lining machine to mark the field (which, in soccer lingo, is known as the "pitch").

Various practice aids are also available. These can play an integral role in developing skills and will be dealt with later when discussing the techniques they are designed to foster.

For now, let's take a look at the basic skills that you will need to play soccer.

Basic Ball Skills

In soccer, there are a number of basic ball skills that you need to master regardless of the position you play. Among these are trapping (the ability to bring a ball under control), dribbling (the art of advancing the ball on the ground with your feet), passing, heading, and shooting.

This chapter will describe the mechanics of these skills. Later, we'll discuss ways of honing the skills in training and how to apply them where you need them the most: in a match.

In essence, there are two ways to play soccer. One is to run like crazy, booting the ball aimlessly and chasing after it. The other approach is to skillfully maneuver and control the ball so that it does the work for you. Because the ball can move faster than any player, and since I've yet to find a ball that is subject to fatigue, you'll encounter more success and better budget your energy if you become master of the ball.

GETTING TO KNOW THE BALL

Your first step is simply to acquaint yourself with the ball. See what happens when you roll it from foot to foot. Note how it reacts when you kick its

Giorgio Chinaglia has the ability to control the ball without looking at it, which allows him to see teammates as they break into the clear.

bottom, its middle, or its top. Observe what you can accomplish by using your instep as opposed to your toes, or the inside of your foot in contrast to the outside.

Before long, you'll have developed a mental list of what part of your body or foot to use to obtain a specific ball movement. Through experimentation, and, yes, a bit more reading, you will come to know that soccer demands hundreds of varieties of skills, each appropriate for specific situations. When you can combine the ability to decide on a split second's notice what technique is appropriate with the ability to execute that maneuver correctly, you will experience the joy of being a skillful and creative soccer player.

Perhaps all this talk of knowledge and skill intimidates you. It shouldn't. First of all, if you are a beginner, most of your peers are probably beginners as well. And chances are, in the past you've used your feet to play kickball, and thus have developed some degree of foot–eye coordination without even knowing it. If not, you'll find it won't take long before you're gaining confidence while improving daily.

Soccer is, after all, a game of kicks. As such, we need to set about learning the various ways you can boot a ball, what is appropriate to which situation, and how to practice to improve. All of that will be covered in the chapters ahead. For now, we'll deal with the basic skills: trapping, dribbling, heading, passing, and my favorite, shooting.

Most soccer instructional books teach the skills in that order, but we're going to start with shooting. Why? Because shooting is so important, so basic —indeed, the promise of being able to propel a ball into the goal is what lures so many of us to this marvelous sport in the first place—that I feel any study of ball skills should begin with the most pleasurable of all skills.

SHOTS AND SHOOTING

The ability to shoot, or "finish," is the one skill that most often separates the winners from the losers. As anyone who has seen a game knows, all the marvelous dribbling, passing, and teamwork in the world will go for naught if the last contact, or "touch," of the ball is inadequate.

Shooting requires equal prowess with both feet. In the cherished and zealously defended area in front of the goal, time and space are at such a premium that the "one-footed" player will likely squander half the opportunities that come his way. With scoring chances being so hard to come by, wasting any is truly a soccer sin. As you watch the game, you will notice that all of its great players are able to strike a ball proficiently with either foot. Learn to do the same. It's a skill that will serve you well through all your soccer-playing years.

There are many different ways of shooting a ball. The most often used, because it can combine power with accuracy, is called the *instep drive*.

The Instep Drive

Just as its name implies, in the instep drive you strike the ball with the portion of your foot that is covered by the shoelaces. By using the instep, you achieve maximum power and accuracy.

To perform an instep drive, approach the ball from a 45-degree angle. Bring your kicking foot backward so that the heel is behind the thigh of your supporting (nonkicking) leg with your toes facing the ground. Plant your supporting foot a few inches to the side of the ball and pointed toward the target area.

As your shooting foot thrusts forward, your body leans forward, too. With your shoulders over the ball, your knee stays in front of your foot until after impact, thus providing both power and a low trajectory to the shot.

As you kick the ball, your toes are still pointed downward, your knee is above the ball, and your eyes are fixed squarely on the impact area (a section of the ball). Just as in golf, if you take your eye off the ball, you'll likely mis-hit the shot.

To obtain maximum power, make your foot literally "drive" through the

When you're performing an instep drive, the upper body leans forward and the knee of the kicking leg is above the ball.

ball. When running toward the target, many great shooters blast the ball with such force that they land on their kicking foot.

The Banana Shot

Sometimes you'll find yourself a considerable distance from the goal, with the keeper having narrowed your shooting angle by coming several yards off the goal line. At such a distance even a well-struck instep drive would be saved. What to do?

Because the goalie is off his line, the smart player dips into his arsenal of alternative shots and chooses the "banana shot," which is soccer's equivalent of a baseball curveball. Also referred to as an "inswinger," this type of kick solves the problem of a reduced shooting angle, in effect by widening the goal.

Let's say you're aiming the shot to the keeper's left (your right). Use your right foot, striking the ball with the inside of the foot, to the upper side of the big toe. Let your kicking foot come *behind* the ball, hitting it on the far right side. This imparts a strong sideways spin on the ball, causing it to curve from right to left—and you hope, around the keeper and inside the goal post.

Since the goalie has lessened the distance between himself and you by coming off his line, don't worry about the shot's speed, or "pace" as it's called. *Accuracy* is your *top* priority. Shoot carefully. Don't try to "kill" the ball. Your knee and shoulders are not quite as far forward as on the instep drive and your foot speed into the kick need not be as great.

The goalpost is a good aiming point for the follow-through. The ball should swerve enough *after* it passes the keeper to produce the desired result.

The Chip Shot

Sometimes in his anxiety to lessen a good shooter's target area, the goalie will overcompensate. By coming too far off the goal line, he leaves himself vulnerable to a chip shot—a dipping shot that flies over his head before dropping underneath the crossbar. A properly struck chip is doubly effective because it *appears* to the keeper as if an instep drive is forthcoming. Like a baseball change-up, it is not detectable until the shot is on its way.

When making a chip shot, your entire prekicking procedure is identical to that for the instep drive, but just prior to impact, your shoulders lean *backward* and your foot moves *ahead* of the knee, with your instep striking the underside of the ball. These techniques give the shot its altitude, or loft. A limited follow-through is used.

As when using a lofted club in golf, "touch" is vital. With continued practice you'll come to know exactly how much pace to impart to the shot so that it clears the keeper's outstretched arms without sailing over the crossbar.

One important rule to remember when calculating the proper altitude and distance for a chip shot is that a ball rolling *toward* you is easy to chip—it requires only a short and effortless leg swing. A ball that is rolling *away* from you, however, is always difficult to loft.

The Outside-of-the-Foot Shot

There are times when disguising a shot's direction until the last instant and keeping the ball on the ground will produce the best result. This is true when you and the keeper are close to each other, especially if you are rapidly advancing toward one another. Then it's appropriate to shoot with the outside of your foot.

The outside of the foot can be used to disguise a shot as well as to impart spin.

As with the instep drive, lean your body forward, but approach the ball straight on with your supporting foot pointed ahead and well to the side of the ball. Your shooting foot's backswing is abbreviated.

For a right-footed shot, strike the left side of the ball. Just prior to the kick, let your foot come across and behind the ball, and find the impact area on the outside of your foot, next to the base of the small toe. Use very limited follow-through and keep your foot close to the ground the entire time.

Because the outside-of-the-foot shot imparts a lot of spin and is easier to keep low, the keeper will find it tough to make the save, and even if he does block the ball, to catch it cleanly. Although the instep drive is more powerful, the outside of the foot can be used from moderate distances, especially if the ball is rolling toward you.

The Volley

Not all balls will neatly arrive at your feet for a shot. Some will be midair crosses (a pass from the sideline toward the middle of the field), while others will be bouncing. Off the former, you can shoot either a header or a volley.

Perhaps the toughest shot to control, the volley is a first-touch kick (you literally kick the ball the moment your foot touches it) that requires timing, power, acrobatics, and split-second execution. There are two variations involved: the *straight-on volley* and the *side* variety.

When running "onto a ball" (that is, preparing to shoot the ball back in

The full volley. Note how the shooter keeps his eyes on the ball, his knee over it, and his toes pointed downward.

The side volley as demonstrated by 1980 NASL Rookie of the Year, Jeff Durgan.
The knee of Jeff's shooting leg is forward, and the bottom half is parallel to the ground prior to impact to ensure a low, powerful shot.

the direction from where it came), your shoulders should be perpendicular to the ball's line of flight and, thus, square to the target.

As with all power-oriented finishes, your knee must be above the ball and in front of your kicking foot until well after impact. This is vital since the volley is the toughest of all shots to keep low.

You must also leap early so that your kicking foot is fully extended prior to impact. Your other leg propels your body off the ground. The instep of your kicking foot makes contact with the ball while your toes are pointed downward. To help keep the shot low, I recommend a limited follow-through.

The most common mistake occurs when the shooter, in an effort to maximize power, neglects the steps necessary to control the shot. The pace of the approaching ball ensures that a well-timed volley will have adequate power. If you're going to be successful shooting a volley, you must concentrate on being accurate.

In contrast, the side volley requires you to impart both power and accuracy. Use it to redirect a cross on the first touch when you lack the time and/or space to trap the ball before shooting.

To strike the ball, you should use your near-sided foot—that is, your leg closer to the side from where the cross originates.

At the start, keep your shoulders, upper body, and hips square to the incoming ball, with your arms slightly extended to the side to aid balance. As the ball arrives, pivot on the ball of your supporting foot, and point it at a spot midway between the incoming ball's path and the target.

Draw back your kicking foot so that your lower leg is parallel to the ground, and keep your knee ahead of your foot until after impact. Your toes should be no more than an inch or two closer to the ground than your heel.

Now, as your shooting leg thrusts forward, your shoulders and supporting foot pivot toward the target (clockwise if using the left foot, counterclockwise for right-footed kicks), and you strike the center of the ball with your instep.

As with the straight-on volley, take care not to fire the shot above the bar. The way to control this shot is to keep your kicking foot parallel to the ground throughout the entire backswing and follow-through.

The Half-Volley

Use this variation of the first-touch shot to strike a ball on the short hop. The closer the ball is to the ground as you kick it, the easier it is to perform the shot correctly.

Lean your body far forward, with your knee well ahead and over the ball, and bring your kicking leg back so it is square to the incoming ball. Once again, kick with your instep, keeping your toes pointed downward the entire time. As you gain proficiency you will learn to thrust your kicking foot with such force that you will actually land on it. Doing so will make you get above the ball early, helping to keep the shots low and powerful.

The Bicycle Kick

At the more advanced levels of soccer, you'll sometimes see players perform a spectacular overhead shot. Known as the bicycle (or scissors) kick, it is used to shoot a high ball on the first touch when the player's back is facing the target.

To perform a bicycle kick, a player moves his nonkicking foot skyward, keeping his leg fairly straight. As the nonkicking foot thrusts upward, the player uses his kicking foot to push his body off the ground. The nonkicking foot lowers as the kicking foot (by now higher than the player's upper body, which is parallel to the ground) smashes, instep first, into the middle of the ball.

On the follow-through, the player's palms are the first parts of his body to make contact with the ground, to cushion the landing, followed by the seat of the pants.

It should be noted that a bicycle kick performed in traffic constitutes a dangerous play. In addition, improper technique can make for uncomfortable landings. As such, I advise younger players and beginners either to forego

The scissors, or bicycle kick: not for the beginning or inexperienced player.

attempting it or to try it while practicing with a knowledgeable coach on a soft surface (such as a gym mat or a sandy beach).

Where to Shoot

All else being equal, low shots are the most troublesome to goalkeepers. However, as noted, you will find yourself in situations where a chip and/or swerving shot are more appropriate.

A shot needn't go directly into the net for it to be successful. A hard kick that the keeper can only parry back into play may yield an empty net opportunity for you or a teammate on the rebound. Because of this, the more acute, or narrow, your angle to the goal, the more important it is to *aim toward the far side of the net*. A near-post shot, even if uncatchable, is easy for the keeper to deflect over the goal line and out of bounds, conceding only a corner kick. By contrast, the same situation on a far-post shot, away from the goalie, yields a great scoring opportunity.

Another factor when deciding where to shoot is the angle of the pass (service). A pass that travels *across* the face of the goalmouth forces the keeper to move rapidly to the side. Many times the goalie won't have time to set himself prior to your shot, especially if the shot is taken on the initial touch. The smart striker exploits the goalie's momentum by aiming his shot in the direction from which the cross comes, that is, *behind* the keeper.

A third consideration involves observation. Does the goalie have a weakness? Many keepers are "one-sided": they dive far more effectively either to their right or their left. By paying attention during the pregame warm-up and during the match, you can often detect a goalie's weakness that you can later exploit.

Overview

The most important quality that all great finishers possess, be they Gerd Mueller, Giorgio Chinaglia, or Pelé, is accuracy. In their anxiety to produce a powerful shot, many players fail to put the ball on net. Always remember: It is far, far better to sacrifice power to accuracy than vice versa.

Perhaps the most common error at all levels of the sport occurs when the shooter chooses the wrong type of shot. When, as the ball arrives, you are so close to the goal or the keeper that an accurate shot with modest pace will suffice, why attempt an instep drive and risk missing the ball entirely? The polished finisher will literally pass the ball into the net, using the inside of the foot. By being alert and thinking ahead you will know which technique to employ when the ball arrives. As veteran NASL and MISL coach Peter Wall notes, "The great strikers never seem to hit the ball any harder than they have to in order to score."

In addition, the truly outstanding goal scorers all *expect* the ball to come to them. They anticipate that a defender's clearance will be miskicked. Whenever, wherever, and however the ball arrives, they are ready to capitalize.

One final point is to look *at* the ball as you strike it, particularly when performing an instep drive, a volley, or a bicycle kick. You should survey the situation, make your decision on which type of shot to use and where to aim, and then concentrate on the mechanics involved.

PASSING

"If you can't pass, you can't play soccer." I don't know how many times that's been said, and trite as it may sound, it's true. After shooting, passing is the next most fundamental skill in soccer.

Although there are many different types of passes, there are some principles that apply to all. To be effective, a pass should be easy for the receiver to control on the first touch. It should be made to a player who is in a better attacking position at the time he receives the ball than was the server when he

When making a push pass, the kicking leg acts as a pendulum, while the supporting foot points toward the target. Note how the entire inside of the foot is used to strike the center of the ball.

made the pass. It must be properly weighted—that is, possess enough pace to reach the receiver quickly—yet be "soft" enough to be controllable.

The Push Pass

The most commonly used and basic service, the push pass is ideal for accuracy over short to medium distances (5 to 30 yards). To perform a push pass, place your supporting foot next to the ball, pointed toward the target. Use your kicking leg as a pendulum, keeping your knee slightly bent, and angle the inside of the foot perpendicular to the target to expose the maximum striking area of your shoe.

As your foot swings through the ball, your heel and toe are equidistant from the ground. Let the inside of your foot hit just above the center of the ball so that the pass will roll—not bounce—and thus be easier for your receiver to control.

The Instep Pass

When passing over a greater distance, use the instep pass. Your technique here is nearly identical with that of the instep drive; the only difference is that you trade ball height for power. You'll achieve a well-lofted pass by leaning backward as you approach the ball. The farther back your shoulders, the greater

The instep pass covers longer distances. The shoulders lean backward so the kicking foot strikes underneath the ball, adding height to the pass.

the altitude of your kick, since leaning back allows your foot to precede the knee, which, in turn, causes the instep to strike the underside of the ball, thus lifting it.

The Chip Pass

When a defender is positioned directly between you and your receiver, you can loft the ball over the defender with a chip pass. Because it requires a great deal

Execute the chip pass with the foot scooping downward, under the ball. The toes jab into the ground with little or no follow-through.

of skill and touch, the chip pass is normally used only at the more advanced levels of the game.

To make a chip pass, approach the ball directly from behind, and bend your kicking leg exaggeratedly at the knee so your foot is brought back behind the thigh. On impact, stab the ball of your kicking foot into the ground, letting your toes kick the underside of the ball. Finish with a short, limited follow-through.

Note that the chip pass is easiest to complete when the ball is rolling *toward* you, and you'll find it virtually impossible to obtain the required height under any other circumstance.

Push Pass (Outside of Foot)

Both in dribbling and passing, the outside of the foot can be put to good use. This is especially true when playing a wall pass (give-and-go) on the first touch over a short distance. This variety of pass can be made without breaking stride.

Use the foot closer to the incoming ball to make the kick. Start by crossing the kicking foot over the supporting foot, bending the leg of the kicking foot slightly at the knee. Then the kicking foot passes back over the supporting foot and toward the ball. Use the entire outside of your shoe to strike the ball just above its center.

The Back Heel

There will be times when you will want to pass the ball backward to a trailing teammate as quickly as possible. This is especially common when you are one of the front-runners on the attack, with offensive help behind you and several opponents ahead. By stepping *over* the ball and passing it back *without breaking stride,* you have put the element of surprise on your offense's side. Further, by passing behind you in a tight situation, you give your receiver more time in which to control the pass and make a constructive judgment as to what to do with the ball.

To make the back-heel pass step over the ball with your kicking foot, and angle your heel below the height of the toe as you start your backswing. Remember, unlike most other kicks, here your heel strikes the ball *during* the backswing. Using your knee as a fulcrum, thrust your foot into the ball just as the foot becomes parallel to the ground.

Keep in mind that the back-heel pass is only effective if your receiver is far enough away from you so that the pass will not take him by surprise (with

The back-heel pass adds an element of surprise to an attacking team's game.

the ball rolling past him before he can react) and yet close enough so that the ball will reach him quickly. Normally a 5-to-15-yard distance is ideal. For easy control, put only a moderate pace on your heel pass, particularly since your receiver will be running toward the ball.

Outside-of-the-Foot Pass for Distance

To make an outside-of-the-foot pass for distance, approach the ball directly from behind, then draw your kicking foot back, with your toes pointing downward. Let your kicking foot come *across* the back of the ball and strike it from the side—at the nine o'clock position with your right foot, the three o'clock position with your left—using the front portion of the outside of your foot. The kicking foot, following through away from the body, imparts a spin on the ball similar to that of a baseball pitcher's screwball.

OPTIONS: WHEN AND WHERE TO PASS

When should you employ these techniques and what options are available? Only when you can properly respond to passing situations under match conditions can you be considered a good passer.

The smart player knows that the best pass is not necessarily one that goes forward. Certainly a penetrating ball that travels past several defenders is a great weapon, and, if the opportunity arises, naturally, you should capitalize on it.

But many times the offensive players who are farthest upfield have neither the time, space, support, nor angle of movement to warrant receiving a pass from you. When this happens, and you do not consider dribbling or shooting to be viable alternatives, you may find it best either to pass the ball backward to a fellow player or "square," that is, parallel, to the goal line.

The Square Ball

Soccer, as you by now have recognized, is a game of angles. Many times a teammate running in the same direction you are and to one side of you will have a better opening in which to dribble, pass, or shoot. As a ball carrier, you must possess the soccer intelligence to know when a teammate is in a better attacking position, and, if he is, then, using one of the passing techniques described above, you should "square" the ball to him to maintain attacking momentum.

The Back Pass

Besides squaring the ball to your left or right, there are two other directions in which you can pass: forward and backward. Obviously, if your team, on offense, is outnumbered in close quarters, it must possess a numerical superiority somewhere else on the field, usually on the weak side or behind the ball. Playing a back pass is the first step toward changing the direction of the attack —that is, moving the play from one side of the field to the other. Following the back pass, your team can complete its change of attack with one long square ball or a series of short ones.

Consider using the back pass also in the defensive half of the field at those times when, if you passed forward or to the side, you'd risk losing possession.

The Through Ball

A penetrating pass that puts several defenders "out of the game" is obviously a great offensive weapon. A through ball is one struck into space behind defenders and in front of a player who sprints onto the pass. Of all the passes, this one requires perfect timing and pace. Passing too hard will cause the ball to be cut out (intercepted) by the sweeper or the keeper, or roll out of bounds over the goal line. Passing without enough pace can result in an interception by a defensive player positioned between you and your intended receiver.

54

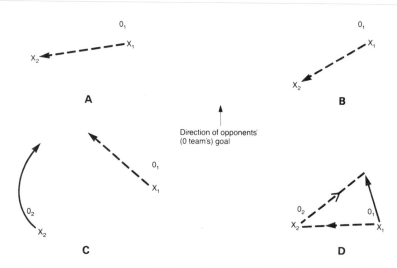

Types of passes: A) square ball, B) back pass, C) through ball, D) wall pass.

Use the through ball to exploit a defense that is "flat" (that is, one in which the defenders are on the same plane). Time the pass so that you kick it as the receiver approaches the final defender. Passing too soon will make it harder for the receiver to get to the ball first, while passing belatedly will result in an offside infraction.

The receiver should be running at about a 45-degree angle to the goal line. If instead he runs straight upfield, he greatly increases the chance that the pace of the pass will be wrong and that the pass will miss him.

The Wall Pass

Also known as the "one-two," the wall pass is soccer's equivalent of basketball's "give-and-go."

Use it when, in possession of the ball, you have a supporting teammate (one near you), you are being challenged by a defender, and there is exploitable space behind that defender. Rather than trying to dribble around the defender, make a pass to the supporting teammate, then run into the space behind your defender to receive a first-touch return pass. Because the defender must complete a 180-degree pivot, you should have no trouble getting behind him after making the initial pass.

You can perform the wall pass using either the inside or the outside of the foot. Most times it's best to use the outside of the foot closer to the receiver because it allows the defender less time to react to make an interception.

The Dummy

One of soccer's most effective "passes," the dummy is made without touching the ball. A potential receiver who is tightly marked (guarded) moves as if to collect a pass, but at the last instant intentionally allows the ball to roll through his legs and on to an open teammate. This "freezes" the defense and throws them off balance.

The wall pass is soccer's version of basketball's "give-and-go." Observe how the return pass is struck into space ahead of the receiver.

The dummy. X1 passes the ball to X2 who is tightly marked but knows that his teammate, X3, is open behind him. He moves toward the ball as if to shoot it on the first touch, but at the last moment opens his legs, and lets it continue to X3. X2's dummy accomplishes several objectives: 1) it draws defenders toward him, 2) it fakes the goalkeeper into moving toward the near post (and perhaps even yards off his line), 3) it causes the player marking X3 to ball-watch as X3 moves in for the shot.

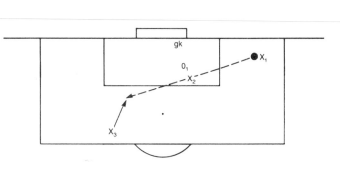

Use the dummy when a teammate is open behind you and is in a better attacking position. This deceptive maneuver is ideal for creating scoring opportunities for attackers behind the ball (known as "withdrawn attackers") in the penalty area (see diagram, page 77).

The Throw-In

A ball that has gone out of bounds can present a splendid passing opportunity to the team that takes possession and makes the throw-in.

To throw a ball back into play you should place your hands on the sides of the ball with your thumbs behind it (see page 21 for the rules governing throw-ins). Like a foot pass, the throw-in is a service directed to another player and, as such, should be easy for the receiver to control.

Many times the flow of play will allow you to see an open teammate or space into which you can place the ball for an attacker to run into. A quickly made throw-in is ideal since it doesn't give the defense time to set up. If, however, you find all your teammates marked, there are different basic plays and types of throw-ins to foil the defense.

A   B   C

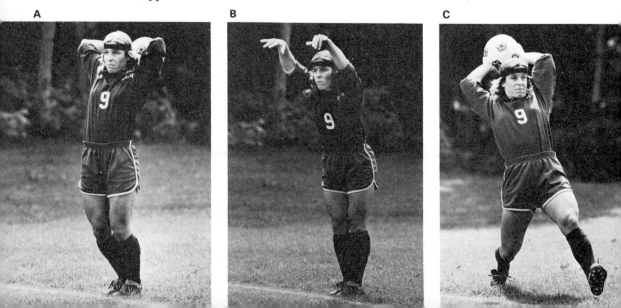

The Check-Off Run

You are the thrower, and your intended receiver, who is closely marked, runs *away* from you. After he has created space behind him, he stops, pivots, and moves back *toward* you into that space to receive the ball.

Down-the-Line Run

An alternative is for all your teammate attackers to vacate the area near the sideline. A withdrawn player then sprints downfield as you lead him with a perfect toss into open space.

The Return Pass

Many times all of your teammates, *except you, the thrower,* are well covered. When this happens, have all but one player run away from the ball. The remaining man gets between his marker and the sideline, receives your toss, and passes the ball back to you on the initial touch. More often than not in this instance, the best throw-in is a high one, and the teammate's return pass will be a header.

Crisscrossing Runs

Interchanging runs, too, can be an effective means of springing an attacker free as she heads toward the opponent's goal line. At the start of an interchanging, or crisscross, run, the two offensive players are tightly guarded. The downfield

When performing a throw-in, use two hands, keep your feet on the ground, and throw from directly overhead (A, B). On a long throw-in down the line (C, D), stride with one foot *prior* to releasing the ball to gain leverage. If either foot leaves the ground during or following the ball's release (E), the throw will be judged illegal and the opposing team will be awarded a throw-in.

D

E

A   B

Off-the-ball movement can free an attacker to receive a throw-in as she moves toward the goal. In this sequence, both potential attackers are tightly marked (A). Number 3 starts the play by running upfield, toward her own team's defensive zone (B). Her move-

player runs toward her teammate, and the marker follows, creating an open space. Approaching her teammate, the second player moves into that gap, and the ball is thrown ahead of her, not to her feet, so that she may receive it as she runs forward on attack.

The Long Throw-In

If your team is awarded a throw-in deep in the attacking third of the field, a long toss can be just as dangerous as a corner kick.

If you are the thrower, by the laws of soccer, you're allowed to run as far as you want before releasing the ball, so long as you don't cross the sideline and you throw the ball from the point where the ball left the field.*

You can improve your throwing distance by incorporating leg power. One way to accomplish this is to throw the ball as you stride with one foot ahead of the other. Bend your front leg at the knee and make your last step a long one. Another way is to thrust your upper body forward as the ball leaves your hands. Soccer laws state that you may land inside the touchline as long as 1) the ball is released prior to your crossing into the playing field, 2) both feet remain on the ground during the toss, and 3) all other regulations are adhered to.

*FIFA laws require only that parts of both feet be on or before the touchline while many youth and scholastic leagues further stipulate that both feet must remain entirely behind the line until the throwing motion is completed.

The impact area for heading a ball, outlined.

| C | D | E |

ment draws her marker with her, thus creating space for attacker #8 to run into (C), (D). Number 8 waits until her teammate's marker approaches, then sprints to collect the ball as it's thrown into dangerous attacking space (E).

HEADING

You're playing defense—or offense—and the ball comes sailing toward you, somewhat higher than your head. You want to pass the ball, or possibly even shoot it. What to do? Answer: Use your head, of course. "My head?" cries the young player in alarm, "won't it *hurt?*" To be sure, no soccer skill is further removed from the mainstream of North American sport than thrusting one's head into a ball. Still, the header is an important soccer weapon and, when taught correctly, is a surprisingly easy, safe, and painless skill to master.

When learning to head the ball, think of the portion of the forehead just under the hairline as the impact area. Keeping your neck still, lean your upper body back from the waist *before* moving forward, so that your head strikes the ball—*not* the other way around!

When heading, keep your eyes open and "throw" them at the approaching ball. Your neck should remain stiff while your upper body thrusts forward so that your forehead propels the ball toward the intended target.

You can use your arms to aid leverage and balance. If you're a beginner, you may wish to place your arms in front of your chest before bringing them backward as the upper body moves forward to strike the ball. This will also improve your timing until the skill becomes second nature.

Always keep your eyes open until the ball is struck. To accomplish this, you must, in effect, *throw your eyes at the ball.* They will automatically close on impact. By following the ball all the way to impact, you will avoid the painful experience of hitting the ball with your nose or the top of your head.

Types of Headers

Generally, there are four reasons to head the ball: to clear a ball from danger defensively, to win a 50-50 ball, to shoot, and to pass.

Defensive Heading

Often performed under extreme duress, the defensive header is used to thwart an opponent's scoring opportunity while clearing the ball from the danger zone in front of one's own goal. Thus, with the defensive header it is desirable to achieve both maximum height and distance.

To head defensively, use your upper body to impart thrust, and strike the underside of the ball with your forehead. Time your leap so that you strike the ball while you're still rising (*not after* you have reached your jump's zenith).

Offensive Heading

There are two types of offensive heading: passing and shooting.

Heading for goal involves the same basic steps outlined above, the only difference being the need to impart maximum power. This is done by leaning backward from the waist as far as possible at the start of the leap before forcefully thrusting your body forward when striking the ball.

The player on the right has just struck a defensive header for height and distance.

There are two reasons, when heading for goal, that you should try to shoot the ball downward not upward. First, the resulting shot will be low and powerful. Second, such a shot will be far more difficult for the goalie to save cleanly. Failing to get *above* the ball before striking its *top* half will result either in a weak shot or one that sails harmlessly over the bar.

When challenged by a defensive player, try to jump *forward,* as well as upward, but be careful not to blatantly barge into your rival lest you be called for a foul.

When heading a pass to a teammate, try to keep the service "soft" so the pass will be easy to receive. If your intended receiver is close to you, let your head absorb the power of the ball by keeping the neck firm and moving your head only a few inches forward when making contact.

The Back Header

A popular weapon on corner kicks and crosses is a short ball played toward the near post. As the defense and the goalkeeper move forward, an offensive player heads the ball backward across the face of the inadequately defended goalmouth.

In essence, the back header changes the ball's path of flight *into* the goalmouth and adds height to the ball's flight. Both are accomplished by hitting the underside of the ball and flicking your head up and backward on impact.

As the ball approaches you, your chin should be touching your chest, with your head lower than the ball's plane of flight. The hairline is used to redirect the ball.

The Flick Header

A variation of the back header, the flick header comes in handy when you redirect the ball only slightly. Also popular on corner kicks and crosses, the flick header can be used after you have made an offensive run diagonally at the near post and you want to aim a shot backward and on goal.

The back header as executed by New York Cosmos and U.S. National Team member Rick Davis (#17). Rick uses the very top of his head to touch the underside of the ball.

University of Vermont star Hilary Engisch shows perfect form executing the diving header.

The speed of the incoming ball provides the power for the shot. Using the part of your forehead closest to the goal line and above the outside part of your eye, flick the ball with your head as the ball travels by. In effect, you are touching the side of the ball with the outside of your forehead.

The Diving Header

There will be times when you need to pass, clear, or shoot the ball on the first touch but it arrives low and some distance ahead of you. By throwing yourself at the ball and using your head to redirect it, you can achieve your objective.

When performing a diving header you must anticipate the height of the ball at impact so as to strike it with your hairline. At that point, your body should be parallel to the ground, your neck stiff, and your hands extended to cushion your landing. (Keep in mind that if you dive near an opponent's feet to head the ball, *you* will have committed a dangerous play, an indirect free kick offense.) Because it demands great skill and timing, the diving header should only be attempted by older and more advanced athletes.

DRIBBLING

Dribbling is the art of advancing the ball upfield with your feet. If you're a good dribbler, you should be able to move nearly as rapidly with the ball as you can without it. You should also be able to withstand the defense's efforts to take the ball from you and feint and dodge with the ball to maneuver around defenders.

Practice using the inside and outside of both feet when you dribble. You'll find that the length of your stride and how and where you touch the ball vary with each situation, but all forms of dribbling require good balance and control.

When to Dribble

In a game, when you have possession of the ball, you're faced with many options. You can clear the ball from danger by booting it upfield or into touch, pass to a teammate, pass to open space, dribble, or shoot.

When should you dribble? As a rule, you should do so 1) when your chances of safely completing a pass to a teammate in a better position are not good, 2) when running into an undefended open area, 3) when you have a defender isolated one-on-one with plenty of prime attacking space exposed behind him, or 4) when successfully dribbling will yield a better shot than that of any teammates who are positioned to receive a pass.

If you're new to the art of dribbling, you'll soon discover that you dribble either *to retain possession of the ball* or *to beat a defender (or defenders)*. In either case, you must always weigh dribbling's potential advantage against the possibility that you may lose the ball.

Never, ever, if you can help it, lose the ball by dribbling in your defensive third of the field or when many of your teammates are in front of you, since in the latter case, you and your team will find yourselves outnumbered if the opposing team steals the ball.

Outstanding dribbling technique. The attacker has placed the ball on the outside of the foot away from his marker while his body acts as a shield. Note how the dribbler's eyes scan the field rather than look at the ball.

Team America veteran Boris Bandov shows how to beat a defender *without* even touching the ball! Boris brings his left foot back, creating the illusion that he will move to his right, but then brings his left foot *over* the ball. By doing so, he "wrong-foots" the

Beating an Opponent

To be a good attacking soccer player you must possess the ability to "take on" opposing players—that is, face them head-to-head and beat them. This skill is particularly important in the offensive third of the field.

Once again, as with other soccer skills, it is vital that you be a good "two-footed player." If you're weak with one foot, an experienced defender will have little trouble forcing you to move to that side.

When trying to beat an opponent, you must always keep the ball closer to your feet than to the defender's nearer foot. In doing so, take short strides and keep the ball in front of you so that, on a moment's notice, you can move in any direction.

Full-speed dribbling requires solid ball control. In this sequence from Soccer Bowl–82, Rick Davis beats two Seattle defenders. After passing the first opponent, Rick switches the ball to his right foot to keep his body between #2 and the ball.

defender, causing him to shift in the wrong direction. Seeing this, Boris now uses the outside of his left foot to push the ball around his man.

Further, as you become an outstanding dribbler, you should be able to fool defenders *without* touching the ball. By dipping your hips and/or shoulders you can give the false appearance of moving the ball in that direction.

Once you've made your move and advanced around the side of the defender, the ball should be on the outside of your foot that is away from the defender. At the same time, you can use your body as a shield so that the defender is unable to touch the ball without fouling.

Dribbling into Open Space

Another form of dribbling is used when you have plenty of open territory in which to advance before a defender challenges you. This will often occur when

your team changes the direction of its attack or if you are an overlapping defender.

When dribbling into open space, push the ball farther in front of you than you would when trying to beat a defender. Dribble the ball with the front of your foot and advance with full strides at maximum speed.

Riding the Tackle

When racing at full speed, you'll often encounter challenges from the side, just as you do when you dribble around an opponent. Usually, the smart defender will lean into you with his upper body to gain leverage and to make you lose your balance. How do you counteract this tactic? Simple. By changing your center of gravity. Shift your body weight *toward* the defender while lowering your shoulder that is nearer to him. If need be, the shoulder can make contact with the defender's upper body while you play the ball with your far-sided foot.

Dribbling to Maintain Possession

There are occasions when you'll "hold" the ball to buy time. This is done when no teammate is open for a pass and there are too many opponents to dribble through.

Shielding

Shielding is the skill of using your body to protect the ball from a defender. Your side or back is to your rival, and you keep the ball on the foot that is away from him. You may extend your arms slightly to maintain balance and improve the shield, but if your arms are raised in an offensive manner (often interpreted by officials to mean near, at, or above shoulder height and/or backward and into the defender), you'll have a foul called on you.

There is a fine line between what constitutes shielding and obstruction. If you have control of the ball or are close enough to play it immediately and are not moving into your opponent, you may legally use your body to help protect the ball. However, if you back into your rival or hinder his progress when contesting a loose ball, you will be guilty of obstruction, an indirect free kick offense. A note of warning: You will be called for obstruction if you interpose your body between the ball and your opponent (or his path) and you do not presently have the capability of playing the ball—even if no contact occurs.

When your back is to your opponent and his goal, and you and your opponent are stationary, try to maintain a low center of gravity by bending your

When receiving a pass with your back to the goal, use your body to shield the defender from the ball. Here, the receiver collects the ball with the foot that is away from the marker and uses his left arm to aid balance and prevent the defender from intercepting. It is illegal to use your arms aggressively to block the defender while shielding (right).

knees and moving your hips backward. You'll find that you can control the ball, while keeping it at maximum distance from the defender, by touching it on top with the sole of your shoe.

At no time should you expose the ball by bringing it too close to your body or between your legs. Doing this gives the defender a chance to poke the ball away with an outstretched toe.

Turning the Defender

Should the defender overplay you when you are shielding with your back to her goal, you can pivot and advance around your rival. This is a great skill to possess, especially if you're a striker, since you'll often receive the ball while facing your own net.

The time to turn is when you can literally *feel* the defender on your back or side, and when there is space behind her to exploit. After you determine which side of your body the defender is on, simply turn the opposite way. If the pressure is exerted on your right side, pivot left, and vice versa. As you turn,

If a defender is too close as you receive a pass, use your body to "turn"—that is, pivot around her.

lower your inside shoulder into the defender while controlling the ball with your outside foot.

You must always be certain that the defender's body is in contact with yours when you begin your pivot. Otherwise, the defender can take a step backward and your turn will thereby expose the ball.

Moving into Space

Frequently when players dribble, they don't realize that space may have been created in the area from which they came. The younger athlete tends to move "full speed ahead," even when a number of opponents are blocking his path to the goal.

A far better alternative is to push the ball with the outside of your foot and circle backward, *away* from the defender. Use your right foot to pivot clockwise, your left foot to pivot counterclockwise. By doing so, you will often be able to shake free from your man for a second, thus allowing you the time and space needed to make a good pass. A good rule to remember when dribbling is *always pivot away from the flow of traffic.*

TRAPPING

You now can kick, shoot, pass, head, and dribble the ball, but how do you stop the ball that is rolling on the ground or flying through the air toward you?

There are several parts of the body that can be utilized to gain control of a moving ball. The ones used most often are the feet, thighs, chest, and head.

The Foot Trap

A ball rolling on the ground or bouncing at your feet can be trapped by using the inside, outside, or bottom of your shoe.

When trapping with the bottom of your foot, keep your heel a couple of inches off the ground and about 4 inches lower than your toes. Trapping this way is particularly useful when you have your back to the defender and you wish to "hold" the ball until support arrives.

When using the inside or outside of your foot, face your body toward the incoming ball and turn your receiving foot inward (or outward) at a 90-degree angle to the approaching ball. Keep your foot a few inches off the ground (so

When using the bottom of your foot to trap a ball, keep your toes a few inches higher than your heel.

The thigh trap. When performed correctly, the receiver can gain immediate control and pass, shoot, or move forward to dribble before the ball touches the ground.

as to touch the middle or upper half of the ball), and "cushion" the ball by moving your foot back slightly on impact. By positioning the knee slightly ahead of the foot as the ball arrives, you will better maintain good, close control of the ball.

The Thigh Trap

The thigh trap is most useful when the ball is dropping toward you and below your waist. Start by squaring yourself to the path of the incoming ball and lift your receiving knee so that your upper leg is at about a 45-degree angle to the ground. The impact area extends from 4 inches above your knee to the top of your leg. As the ball arrives, move your knee downward. On impact, withdraw the knee to cushion the ball so that it will land in front of your receiving leg, where you can play it immediately.

The Chest Trap

You can use your chest to control either a bouncing or a dropping ball.

To trap a ball that's dropping, lean your body back from the waist, extending your arms to the side to aid leverage.

As the ball strikes your chest, hold your breath and let your upper body cushion the ball. When the ball leaves the chest, lean your body forward so that you're ready to advance the ball as soon as it hits the ground. If you're an accomplished athlete, you should be able to strike the ball on the volley (in the

There are two types of chest traps. Hilary, left, leans backward to cushion a ball that is descending. By contrast, YMCA coach Mark Lukas leans forward and over a ball that is rising. By doing so, he directs the ball downward and onto his feet.

air) after chesting it by using either the inside or the instep of the foot.

When running onto a bouncing ball, try to lean your upper body forward and *over* the ball. That way, the ball is forced downward, onto the feet and, when performed properly, you won't have to break stride.

The Head Trap

Of all the traps, the head trap takes the longest time from the initial touch to the moment of complete control, so use it only when there are no defenders nearby.

Your head should hit the nearside and underside of the ball, and withdraw on impact. To further soften the touch, lean your body backward.

If you're going to be a good soccer player, you must come to possess a fundamental grasp of the basic ball skills. The mark of an accomplished performer is his ability to do things on the first touch that most others require two or three touches to accomplish. The exceptional player rarely loses control of the ball; he is its master.

Whatever you seek to accomplish on the field will be predicated on your ability to make the ball do what you want it to do. As soon as you learn to manipulate the ball without having to look at it, you can experiment and come to enjoy the creative aspects of the game. Although soccer is a team game, there is plenty of room for the virtuoso whose ability to produce magic with a ball is as entertaining to fans as it can be helpful to his team.

Off-the-ball supporting is a vital part of attacking soccer. As Julio Cesar Romero (#7) breaks free of his marker, Giorgio Chinaglia (#9) runs away from the penalty area and toward Romero. This forces Chinaglia's marker to vacate the prime scoring zone and gives Romero a teammate, Chinaglia himself, to pass to.

Offensive Movement

Since most soccer games consist of 90 minutes' playing time, twenty-two participants, and one ball, the average player spends less than 5 minutes in possession. Therefore, what he does the other 85-plus minutes is extremely important.

To be a good offensive soccer player, you need to move intelligently at all times—and that means coordinating your own movements with those of your teammates. The ability to think and move collectively is what allows the outstanding teams to advance the ball upfield through a series of simple passes with a minimal risk of losing the ball.

Off-the-ball movement—that is, movement by an attacking player not in possession of the ball —is generally instituted to get open for a pass or to create space for teammates. Also, off-the-ball movement forces defenders into making decisions, and the more decisions a defender must make, the greater the likelihood he will make at least a few incorrect ones.

The intelligent attacker knows how to confuse opponents. Here's a hypothetical example. The Ft. Lauderdale Strikers are advancing the ball against the Chicago Sting. Sting stopper Rudy Glenn has been given the specific assignment of

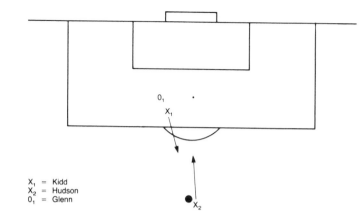

X_1 = Kidd
X_2 = Hudson
0_1 = Glenn

marking forward Brian Kidd. Wherever the always dangerous Kidd goes, Glenn follows. With only the sweeper and the goalkeeper behind him, Glenn has a tough assignment.

On this specific play, Kidd is perched at the top of the penalty area as teammate Ray Hudson dribbles across the 35-yardline and toward the goal. Instead of moving into the box, Kidd sprints toward Hudson (see diagram).

If Glenn follows Kidd, he will leave a dangerous amount of prime attacking space open behind him. To create a good scoring opportunity, all Hudson needs to do is pass the ball to Kidd, who would then strike a wall pass back to Hudson or simply dribble past his man. On the other hand, if Glenn leaves Kidd, he allows a world-class player to receive the ball, turn, and run at him.

What should Rudy Glenn do? To make the right decision he must know if the sweeper is in a good central position to back him up, how many Ft. Lauderdale players are attacking as opposed to the number of Sting athletes in defensive positions, how good a finisher Hudson is, what the other Striker players are doing, and his own strengths and weaknesses. Based on all this data, he must decide, and decide correctly, on a split-second's notice. Even if he makes the right choice but hesitates in doing so, he will invite trouble.

If, on offense, Brian Kidd can vary his runs throughout the match—sometimes as a target for a pass, sometimes as a decoy—sooner or later even the most experienced defender will be drawn out of position. That's why Concordia College coach Lou Gallo often admonishes immobile players to "do something, even if it's wrong." At the very least, movement by attackers begets movement by defenders. And when defenders run, they often leave holes that withdrawn offensive players can exploit.

There are times when players run *away* from the play. They do this to draw defenders after them, thus making space for teammates to utilize.

Let's say, for example, that the attacking right midfielder has dribbled around his marker and is now headed upfield just inside the sideline. The only players between him and goal are a teammate (the right wing) and an opponent who is marking the wing.

When the winger runs to the middle of the penalty area, he forces his marker to follow, since the defender cannot allow an attacking player to run free in front of the net. Thus, an entire alley inside the sideline is now open for the ball carrier to exploit. (See diagram: "Running to the Middle to Create Space.")

Similarly, when an attacking midfielder has dribbled unmarked up the middle of the field, the striker runs toward the sideline at a diagonal. After clearing his marker from the central zone, the striker can either check back for a pass or keep moving to allow a teammate to run behind him. (See diagram: "Running toward the Sideline to Create Space.")

Creating Space

Running toward the middle to create space. X1, the winger, runs into the penalty area, and O1, who's been marking him, follows. Now X2, the ball carrier, has the entire right side of the field open, into which he can advance.

Running toward the sideline to create space. X1 has beaten O1, who is chasing from behind. As X1 approaches, X2 runs away from the play. If O2 follows, X2 keeps moving. Otherwise, X2 can move toward X1 to support. Note that X3 does not begin his move too soon. Instead, he times his run so that O3 does not have a chance to intercept the path of X1.

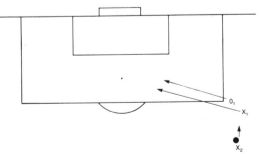

RUNNING TOWARD THE MIDDLE TO CREATE SPACE

RUNNING TOWARD THE SIDELINE TO CREATE SPACE

STAYING WIDE

Sometimes a player can aid his team's attack simply by remaining away from the action.

Ideally, the offensive team wishes to create small-sided confrontations in the penalty area. It is far easier to score in a 2-versus-2 situation than a 5-versus-5 match-up.

The offensive team's objective is to give its shooters maximum time and space. Therefore, an offensive player should not move toward the goal and enter into the penalty area unless he has the ball or is unmarked. (Unless, as noted on page 28, you are the striker serving as a target player.) By remaining wide or upfield, he hopes to keep a defender away from the goalmouth.

The outside midfielder and forward on the weak side should stay as close to the sideline as possible. This will either spread the defense or cause the weak-side defender to temporarily forget his assignment. A weak-side attacker can always run onto the ball if he is wide.

How many times have potentially dangerous crosses sailed just past the far post and over all of the attackers? If the winger had remained wide and not begun his run toward the goal until *after* the cross was struck, he would have enjoyed a great scoring opportunity.

Here, #18 runs to an outside supporting position. Now his teammate can advance the ball upfield to him with an easy rather than a difficult pass.

The knowledge of how to move into supporting positions is vital if a team is to advance the ball upfield without incurring unnecessary risks. Proper support not only gives the ball carrier more options, it also allows him to make simpler, safer passes.

The term "running to support" simply means making yourself available for a pass. When you're a potential receiver, you should remember that it is far easier for a teammate to make a short pass than a long one, to play the ball in the direction that he is facing, and to pass to a player who is moving toward the ball instead of away from it.

SUPPORTING FROM BEHIND

Many times the ball carrier, especially when he's in the offensive third of the field, will find his path to the goal well defended. Rather than trying to dribble through an army of opponents or attempting a low-percentage penetrating pass, he can be provided with a better alternative if a withdrawn attacking player intelligently moves into a *rear supporting position.*

As the diagram illustrates, the supporting player will have many good options after receiving the ball.

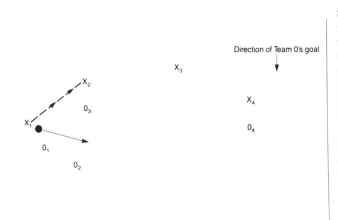

Direction of Team O's goal

Supporting from behind. X1 has nowhere to go—he is marked by O1, who is supported by the sweeper, O2. A simple back pass opens up a range of options for the receiver, X2. He can dribble to his right (down the line) into space cleared by X1's run; he can play a square ball (see page 53) to teammate X3 or a penetrating ball to a front-runner. Remember, since defenders try to stay between the ball and the goal (and thus might be deeper than the ball's original position when held by X1), the supporting players are likely to be unmarked.

When supporting from the rear, you should be at least 5 and no more than 15 yards from the ball. If you are closer, the player who is defending against the ball carrier can slide over quickly to tackle you, even before you've gained control. At the same time, supporting at too great a distance allows defenders off the ball to shift their positions to cover attackers that the receiver could otherwise consider prime targets.

You should provide rear support from an angle toward the middle of the field. When the defender who is marking the ball carrier is unsupported, it will be easy for you, as receiver, to strike a penetrating wall pass for the original ball carrier to run onto. Offensive supporting from an inside angle brings you closer to potential receivers for your passes. It also gives you a better line of vision to see the ball, the space in front, and the surrounding players.

THE CHECK-OFF RUN

Any youngster who has played touch football is familiar with a pass pattern known as the "buttonhook." In soccer, the same movement is referred to as a "check-off run." After moving away from the play, the potential receiver stops, turns, and comes back to meet the ball carrier.

Passing to a receiver who has completed a properly timed and executed check-off maneuver has many advantages. First, the defender will be behind the receiver, so the risk of an interception is reduced. Second, the ball can be played to the receiver's feet. Third, by shielding his marker off the ball, the receiver will have time to maintain possession. Fourth, the receiver will be facing most of his teammates, so he should have plenty of good passing options. Finally, there will be space created behind the receiver that can be exploited through use of a wall pass.

After playing the ball to a teammate who has made a check-off run, the passer immediately moves ahead for a possible return feed.

Angles are important. The player making the check-off run should be downfield and at least slightly to the side of the ball carrier. If he is directly in line with the ball carrier and the ball carrier's defender, it will be far more difficult for the passer to get the ball to him.

It is important that the receiver continue to move toward the ball after the pass is struck. Should he stop and wait for the ball to arrive, the defender can advance past him to make the interception. As long as the receiver is moving

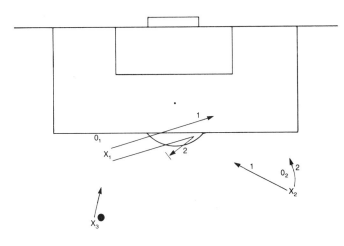

The check-off option. The diagram shows a typical check-off situation. X3, the ball carrier, is unmarked. X1, the striker, runs to create space (option 1). If defender O1 follows him, X1 keeps running away from the ball to create space for X3 to exploit. X2 can then run into a supporting position while being careful to remain far enough from X3 not to allow defender O2 to mark both attackers at once. Should O1, however, *not* follow X1, then X1 can check back into a supporting position, ideal for working a wall pass with X3 while X2 may opt to make a far-post run that would put him in good position for a pass or to get a rebound from X3's shot. X2 is careful not to advance into an offside position.

toward the ball, the referee is less likely to interpret his shielding technique as obstruction.

The check-off run is most often used by forwards who are tightly marked. Although it can be effective at any time or place, it is an especially attractive option in the attacking third of the field.

INTERCHANGING RUNS

Interchanging (crisscross) runs are made in front of the ball by two or more attackers, usually forwards.

The 1981 NCAA Division I champion University of Connecticut Huskies did a great job of incorporating such movement into their game plan. Whenever a midfielder was dribbling across the width of the field, the front-runners would switch positions. Thus, if midfielder Bill Morrone was moving to his left, the team's left wing (Elvis Comrie) would run to the middle of the field just as the striker (Graziano Cornolo) would run parallel to the ball carrier. Comrie's movement created space into which Cornolo could advance. And Morrone could play the ball forward without having to get it by any defenders first.

Interchanging runs can also be made at 45-degree angles as the ball is advanced straight upfield.

The beauty of the crisscrossing configuration is the decoy's success in drawing his marker, which gives the receiver plenty of room in which to work after he gathers in the pass.

DIAGONAL RUNS

When playing a penetrating ball—that is, a downfield ball that goes past one or more defensive players before reaching the receiver—it is far easier for both the passer and the receiver if the latter is running at a diagonal. One popular expression, usually couched in locker-room lingo, states that a player is in trouble if he has the ball and all he can see before him are his teammates' elbows and backsides.

Diagonal runs are often utilized by strikers—most notably, all-time NASL scoring king Giorgio Chinaglia—and when executed properly, they are very difficult to counteract. Chinaglia has an uncanny ability to anticipate just when the ball carrier will break free (and, therefore, when he'll be able to pass). Chinaglia times his run so that he will arrive at the optimum spot for a shot just as the ball is being sent his way.

Unlike many lesser strikers, Chinaglia fully understands that stationing himself in the penalty area *before* the ball arrives hinders his chances of scoring. By arriving prematurely, a forward takes his marker in with him, and once in the box, he has little room to maneuver without moving away from the goal. The alternative—standing still—is equally abhorrent since an immobile striker is an easy player to mark.

Among youth-league and high-school forwards there is a temptation, rarely resisted, to head directly for the goalmouth when their team has the ball.

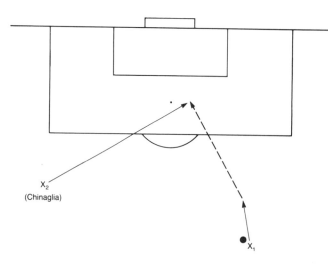

Giorgio Chinaglia's diagonal run.

It's not unusual to find an entire frontline racing for the same area long before the ball can possibly be played into the box. As a result, when the ball does arrive, the goalmouth resembles Grand Central Station at rush hour. Remember: *The less open space, the harder it is for the offense to prevail.*

In contrast, Chinaglia's "patented" diagonal run owes much of its success to the Cosmos' collective off-the-ball intelligence. As the play develops, Giorgio is often out of the picture, with his mates careful to avoid the areas he wishes later to exploit. Chinaglia usually lurks on the weak side. As the ball comes down the right flank, he is to the left of the penalty area and about 20 to 30 yards upfield from the goal line. From there, he can read the play.

His movement has already caused the opposition stopper to leave space behind. The greater the space, the more room and time Chinaglia will have to collect a penetrating pass and to shoot. If the other New York forwards and midfielders seem likely to use that space constructively, Chinaglia is content to stay wide, thus keeping one or more defenders away from the goalmouth.

NEAR-POST RUNS

Another variety of the diagonal run can be made when the ball carrier is wide and near the goal line. Starting from between the top of the box and the penalty spot, a potential receiver runs at a 45-degree angle toward where the near post and 6-yardline intersect.

The runner wants to be just inside the post and about 6 yards in front of

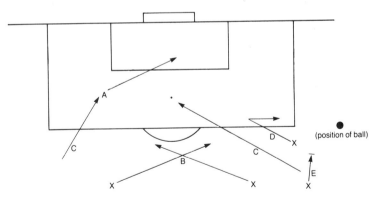

Five types of offensive runs. A) The near-post run. B) Interchanging runs. C) The far-post run. D) The check-off run. E) Running to support the player with the ball.

the goal line as the ball arrives. He must time his move correctly, which is accomplished by estimating how long it will take the ball carrier to break free of his marker before crossing the ball, preferably at head height.

BLIND-SIDE RUNS

When the ball is wide, defenders are faced with a considerable challenge. They must be aware of what is happening at the point of attack while continuing to mark a specific rival.

Forwards can turn this situation to their advantage by positioning themselves at or beyond the far side of the net. Since a defender must stay between the goal and his assigned foe, he will be unable to watch the ball and his man simultaneously. As the defender "ball-watches," the attacker can get an undetected head start. Only the offensive man has full vision.

St. Louis–born Steve Moyers is an excellent example of a striker who runs past defenders and toward the opening at the far post. A tremendous force in the air, Moyers has movements that leave him in perfect position to run onto the ball to drive a header into the net.

OVERVIEW

Many of the greatest goal scorers of all time weren't extraordinarily quick, and their passing and dribbling skills were only good, not great. What has made Gerd Mueller and Giorgio Chinaglia soccer legends in their own time is a combination of knowledge of the game, anticipation, and the finishing ability to capitalize on half-chances with one lethal kick of the ball.

Even if a player can't hit a volley like Mueller, he can still be a high scorer *if* his off-the-ball running is intelligent. Of equal importance, such movement isn't restricted to forwards. *All* players must run smartly to create openings that give the ball carrier several alternatives from which to choose.

This requires team understanding. If two players make similar runs, they succeed only in eliminating themselves from the play. Players off the ball must make complementary runs: some moving to support the ball carrier, others to create space, while still others must think several steps ahead to be open for the second or third pass.

Remember, the attacking team's objectives are:

1) To support the ball carrier so that he has many options and can advance the ball without having to execute a difficult pass or to dribble when outnumbered.

2) To pull defenders *away* from the prime attacking zone in front of the goal.

3) To move into that zone only when in possession of the ball or if unmarked when the ball carrier is in position to pass.

If you're a young player, you may find all this talk about soccer offense complex, overwhelming—and you're right, it is. That's why nine-year-olds playing full-sided games may not be such a good idea.

For those of you who are engaged in full-sided play, be you youngsters or pros, there are several team training tools that can help you and your teammates learn how best to interact. Discussion of team drills and team play can be found in Chapter 8.

4

Defense

Defense is soccer's great equalizer. A team that is fundamentally sound and well organized can be competitive, even if it has considerably less natural ability than its opponents. As with good offense, good defense requires a combination of individual ability fitted to an eleven-player unit.

Usually when we think of defense in soccer, our first image is of a spectacular sliding tackle, or of a sweeper reading the play perfectly before cutting in front of a potential receiver to intercept a pass. Most of the time, though, good defense is far less glamorous: A defender tracks down an opponent, forces the ball carrier to move away from the penalty area, or simply remains goalside of the player with the ball. *Good defense is denial: refusing to permit the attackers to do what they want when they want.* It involves making an opponent use his weaker foot or not allowing him to turn with the ball after he has received it while facing his own goal.

Although to be a good defender you need certain physical attributes, such as a reasonable amount of quickness, it is primarily your mental components that will allow you to excel. Sound judgment and analytical ability are vital, and so is patience.

85

The consummate sliding tackle as performed by University of Connecticut midfielder Billy Morrone (left).

Through good marking position, #3 forces the offensive player to pass backward.

MARKING

Marking involves two situations: guarding a player 1) when he's off the ball, and 2) when he has possession.

When marking the ball carrier, always position yourself between your man and the goal. Your stance should be balanced, allowing you to move in any direction on an instant's notice. Spread your feet to about the same width as your shoulders, with your body bent slightly from the waist and knees. Even when backpedaling, lean your upper body forward and run on the front portion of your feet.

Your distance from the ball is critical. As a marker, you want to be close enough to pounce on any mistake yet have enough space to react to a change of direction and to protect against the offense's give-and-go weapon, the wall pass. Your optimum distance from the ball varies depending primarily on the ball carrier's skill and running pace. The more talented the opponent, and/or the faster he is moving, the more "respect" you must show. Of all these variables, pace should be considered first.

Because it's impossible to backpedal as fast as your opponent can sprint forward, when defending you are at the mercy of an opponent who is in full flight. About all you can do is line up on a plane with the attacker's inside shoulder (the shoulder closest to the center of the field) and force him wide. By using the touchline as an "extra defender," and jockeying the ball carrier so he moves away from his offensive support, you may cause him to run out of space. *At that point,* he *must* change direction. At that point, too, you have slowed his pace, allowing you to close the gap.

An attacker's skill is another factor you must consider. No marker in the world wishes to challenge a great dribbler to a one-on-one confrontation in the open field. Instead, you must deny your rival the most direct route to the goal while simultaneously slowing him down. The latter is accomplished by maintaining an adequate distance (approximately 2 to 3 yards). This prevents the attacker from getting around you and forces him to keep the ball close to his feet (thus making him take shorter strides that decrease his pace).

A large part of deciding how to react to specific game situations lies in evaluating the opponent, the number of offensive and defensive players who are free to help, and the area of the field in which the confrontation is occurring.

Should the dribbler lack teammates to pass to, and you are covered by support from the rear, take a calculated risk and try a tackle. At such moments, a tackle with only an even chance of success is a good gamble. If, however, the attacker has the deck stacked in his favor, you must restrain yourself from tackling unless you are positive you will succeed.

There is nothing more exciting to the fan, or terrifying to a defender, than watching a great dribbler in action. Although a Pelé or a George Best only comes along once in a generation, many teams feature fine dribblers. As a rule, the attacking midfielder and wingers are likely to be the most advanced in this regard, which means that fullbacks and the defensive midfielder must be adept at containment. The more space the attacker has *and* the faster he is moving toward his intended target area as he collects the ball, the more effective he will be. A well-accepted soccer adage implores defenders to force dribblers to "beat you with skill, not with speed."

You can do this in a number of ways. First, if possible, deny the dribbler the ball. Second, if you are unable to prevent him from gaining possession, make sure he receives the ball either as he is stationary or is facing away from where he wants to go. Finally, "force" him *away* from offensive supporting players and *toward* supporting defenders and/or the sideline.

DENYING THE BALL

Even a Pelé or Best can't inflict damage without the ball. (Although, through intelligent off-the-ball movement, a Pelé or Best *can* draw markers into disadvantageous positions to create prime attacking space for themselves or others to exploit.) To "track down" a player of such caliber for 90 minutes is an exhausting experience, both physically and mentally. The harder one works at denying such players possession, the greater the energy expended.

A common tendency among overeager markers is to stay "inside the opponent's shirt" the entire match. This is not only a waste of precious energy, it's also the number one mistake that allows an opponent to get behind his marker before he receives the ball.

The distance between the defender and the attacker is determined by the position of the attacker vis-à-vis the ball and the goal. The longer it will take for the offensive team to get the ball to him, the greater the distance should be.*

By maintaining a considerable distance (up to 10 yards) from the attacker, you can momentarily take your eye off your man to see what is happening around the ball. This 10-yard buffer zone prohibits the offensive player from getting behind you while your attention is temporarily elsewhere. The closer the offensive player is to you, the greater the danger of his running by you when you're not looking. This is called a blind-sided run. You should always position yourself in the attacker's path to the goal.

As the time it will take to get the ball to the attacker lessens, you must narrow the gap. If you don't you allow the opponent to collect the ball with a full head of steam.

If you have defensive support available (that is, an extra defender who has no marking responsibility), you can try to "front" your opponent. By positioning yourself on the side of the attacker closer to the ball while slightly downfield (to prevent a through pass), you hope to discourage the pass. You must take care when fronting, though. Because you are between your man and the ball, you will be unable to see both. Your man can make a run to your blind side, receive a pass, and be on his way to the goal before you know what has happened. That is why, when fronting, it is vital that you have defensive support.

FORCING THE ATTACKER

There will be times when you may actually be able to win the ball. Most of the time, however, playing defense involves denying your opponent time and space. It may not be necessary to try to win the ball (which always involves risk-taking) if the ball carrier can be pressured into making mistakes in judgment and/or execution. It's worth noting that *defensive pressure is not necessarily a physical phenomenon. Rather, it is what the ball carrier perceives.* If you can convince your rival that he is about to be tackled, the ball carrier may rush his

---

*The time it takes to get the ball to a player is determined by the overall skill of the attacking team, the distance from that man to the ball, the amount of congestion around the receiver (if crowded, it will be necessary to make several short passes to get him the ball rather than to play one long service), and whether the ball carrier is unmarked (and, thus, able to pass the ball immediately).

movements and lose control. You can do this by feigning a tackle. Step forward and lower your shoulder. As the offensive player reacts, take a step back to give yourself room to work in.

Aggressive defense can catch attackers by surprise. Instead of the player in possession dictating play, the ball carrier finds himself reacting to the marker's movements. It is amazing how many times outstanding defenders win the ball for their team *without* having to make a tackle or an interception.

Another ploy is to "jockey" the ball carrier. As you mark, assume an open stance to the inside of the ball carrier. Your inside leg should be a foot closer than your outside leg to the opponent and farther from your own goal line, so that your body is at a 45-degree angle to your man. By standing a yard or two downfield of your opponent, you deny your rival the option of beating you to the center of the field and/or dribbling onto his preferred foot.

PREVENTING THE TURN

There will be times when an offensive player receives a service while facing his own net. This is particularly common among strikers, who are masters at collecting a ball, turning sharply, and advancing past their marker for a shot on goal.

Defenders, most often stoppers, must, whenever possible, prevent an opponent from turning in the offensive third of the field. The attacker will turn if he can feel body contact or if he has nobody nearby who is open for a pass. As a marker, you should analyze this latter possibility. A favorite attacking maneuver is one in which a withdrawn player works a penetrating wall pass by using the striker, whose back is to the goal. If you see a potentially damaging give-and-go developing, you may have to gamble by sliding to cover the side that the receiver is moving toward for the return pass.

By "jockeying"—that is, overplaying a foe—defenders can force ball carriers to dribble *away* from the most dangerous attacking area and/or onto their weaker foot.

The tackle. The defender (left) leans his shoulders forward, and the inside of his tackling foot "locks" behind the center of the ball.

If, however, such a threat does not exist (or if you have a supporting defender behind you who can cover the potential receiver should he break through unmarked with the ball), preventing the turn is important.

When marking, you can prevent a turn by standing a yard or two behind the attacker and slightly to the side of his favored foot (or, if he is to the side of the field, between him and the goal). As the attacker pivots, move laterally so that the ball carrier actually "tackles himself"—i.e., runs into you. Care must be taken not to be too close to the attacker lest he be allowed to lower his shoulder and use his body to shield the ball.

A clever decoy involves fooling the attacker into thinking that you're too close. First, make light contact with your man just before the ball arrives. Knowing that the attacker will try to turn on the first touch, you immediately take a step backward and to the side. Should the attacker turn, he will play the ball right into your feet.

TACKLING

Tackling in soccer is the art of dispossessing an attacker of the ball. It can involve poking the ball with your outstretched toe or using your entire body against your opponent.

Although a certain amount of contact is legal when touching the ball first,

when tackling you must always be perceived to be playing the ball and not your opponent. You cannot use your hands or arms to gain an advantage.

There are various types of tackles, depending on the angle of pursuit and the desperation of the moment.

The Front Tackle

When tackling straight on, your shoulder and distribution of body weight are critical elements. As you begin the tackle, the opposite shoulder from your tackling foot leans forward toward the attacker's chest. Most of your weight is on the nontackling foot. This transfers body weight forward, allowing you to gain leverage. The *inside* of your tackling foot makes contact with the ball, and your tackling leg is behind the middle of the ball to prohibit the offensive player from lifting the ball over the tackling foot.

The motion of the tackling foot is downward. Let your leg "lock" into the ball without following through. If your body weight is distributed properly, there is little danger of leg or foot injury.

Tackling from the Side

When challenging from the side, both you and the offensive player are running in the same direction, so it is virtually impossible for you to gain control of the ball. You must therefore be content to redirect the ball so that the attacker overruns it.

You'll find the side tackle most useful when near the sideline, when desperately trying to prevent a shot, or when there is a free teammate to whom you can play the ball.

There are two options at your disposal. You can use the outside of the foot that is closer to the ball carrier; or you can slide across his path, using the inside of the far foot to nick the ball away. In both cases, lean toward your opponent. You can play your shoulder against his to gain leverage as you play the ball.

The Sliding Tackle

The most daring and exciting defensive maneuver is the one you should employ least. The sliding tackle, even when performed correctly, leaves you flat on your back and therefore temporarily out of the play. Use it primarily when you *must* win the ball or otherwise face dire consequences: such as when you are beaten, have no support, and the attacker is advancing goalward. You may also attempt it when the situation is at the opposite extreme: Your team's defense has the attackers well outnumbered so that an unsuccessful slide tackle will not prove costly.

When attempting a sliding tackle, you *must* play the ball and you *cannot* slide from the rear. Failure to heed these regulations is not only punishable by a direct free kick, it is almost always accompanied by a yellow card.

Begin your move when you are in front of the ball carrier and slightly to his side. As you leave your feet, your nontackling foot is the one closer to your opponent. Let your tackling foot come *across* the ball to sweep it away from (not into) the attacker's body.

As in all forms of tackling, timing is vital. You must begin your move just after the dribbler has advanced the ball forward. If you commit to the tackle *as* the attacker is in contact with the ball, the offensive player can push the ball ahead and leap over you, and you are then out of position.

Remember always to come *across* the ball. Many tacklers make the mistake of sliding into the ball, hitting it into the dribbler's legs. This causes the ball to rebound into the path of the offensive player.

TEAM DEFENSIVE SKILLS

Defense is a team proposition. Its basic precepts are simple, most involving little more than hard work and common sense.

The most important equation is numerical: the need to have more of your team's defenders between the ball and your own goal than there are opponents in attacking position. Other team fundamentals derive from individual principles: staying between your man and the goal; being aware of the position of the ball, the net, and the player you are marking; communicating; and not only being ready to cover for any teammates' errors but also anticipating them.

Team Coverage

Defensive alignment is dictated by whether the numerical equation is positive. Under most circumstances, the defensive team should have at least two extra players (the sweeper as well as the goalkeeper) between their goal and the ball.

The most common exception occurs when an errant pass, particularly a square or backward service by a midfielder or defender, is intercepted. This creates a situation in which a team's transition from offense to defense is hampered by having many players caught upfield and therefore out of position. What results is a small-sided confrontation where the defense is often outnumbered with a lot of space behind them for the attackers to utilize.

Defenders must be as cognizant of protecting prime attacking space as they are of covering men, especially when outnumbered. Obviously, if four defenders try to mark man-to-man against six attackers, two players will be unguarded.

Since good defense is, by definition, denying attackers as much space and time as is feasible, the four backs try to concede as little as possible. Their best alternative is to assume central positions, staying behind the ball. Unless the offense's execution breaks down completely, it is unlikely that the defense can regain possession. In fact, if the attackers are competent, it may be impossible to prevent a shot on goal.

What good defensive work *can* prevent is yielding a high-percentage shot from a central position within the penalty area. By making the shooter kick the ball from an angle while under pressure, the defense reduces the likelihood of a score.

To accomplish this, one defender marks the ball carrier. By overplaying the attacker, he hopes to force a nonpenetrating pass in a specific direction. All but one of the remaining defenders, having read their teammate's marking angle, are toward the side of the field to which the ball will be played. They are well behind the play, to prevent a penetrating pass, especially if there is considerable unmanned space between them and the penalty area. Once the initial pass is made, a second defender tries to force the new ball carrier even wider.

Four defenders plus the goalkeeper versus six attackers (4 vs. 6). X1 is the ball carrier. Note how O1, through excellent positioning, "forces" the play so that X1 cannot pass to X2. On the other side of the field, O2 blocks the paths of X4 and X6 and is ready to mark whichever receives a pass. O3 and O4, meanwhile, act as sweepers. O3 is to the inside of X4 and X6. If either gets a pass, O3 can force them wider.

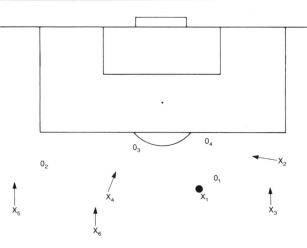

If the defenders can make their adversaries go *around* instead of *through* them, they will realize three primary objectives. First, the number of passes will be greater, as will the time needed to complete all of them. This may give other members of the defending team enough time to get back in the play and provide cover in the middle or the weak side of the field. Second, by keeping the ball on the periphery, all defenders can maintain useful positions in relation to their opponents and the ball. Finally, any shots allowed will come from as acute an angle as possible or, to get a good shot, the attackers will have to play a long cross.

The key ingredient is to defend intelligently. When outnumbered, defenders must not challenge for the ball unless they are confident they will win it or are forced to do so as a last resort. By overplaying the ball carrier, the marker has eliminated half of his opponent's options. That is, by not allowing the attacker to pass to his right, the defender has temporarily eliminated all the offensive players on the right side from the attack. This can turn a four-versus-six disadvantage into a three-on-four situation, with the ball moving *away* from the center of the field. If the attackers are to exploit their numerical advantage on the weak side of the field, they must either make a number of passes (which is time-consuming) or cross the ball over several defensive players (which requires great skill, thus increasing the chance the pass will go awry).

On quick counterattacks, defending territory is as important as marking offensive players. After a turnover, the defense's first priority is to get behind the ball. The second most important consideration is to concentrate defensive pressure and manpower on the center of the field and at the point of attack. Defensive depth is important, too, since a through ball to an onrushing opponent is one of the offense's prime weapons in such situations.

Proper jockeying can also force a ball carrier to "tackle himself." In this sequence, the defender on the left overplays the ball carrier so that he has no choice but to dribble toward the supporting defender and into the defensive team's trap.

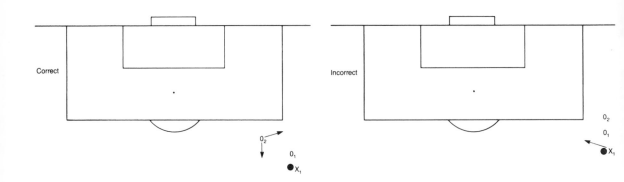

Correct and incorrect defensive supporting.

Correct: X1 is the ball carrier, O1 is the marker; O2 is the supporting defender. O2, positioned at perfect depth and angle, can move to either side should O1 be beaten.

Incorrect: O2 is on a line with O1 and X1. Should X1 beat his man (as shown), he will be between O2 and the goal.

Supporting

Just as the offense wishes to isolate a defender in a two-on-one confrontation, so does the defense hope to enjoy a similar numerical edge.

During the course of a match, it is common for the defense to enjoy at least a one-outfield-player advantage, particularly when the ball carrier has most of his teammates behind him.

The first defender marks the ball carrier. The extra man (the supporter) provides cover. He is positioned approximately 5 yards from his teammate and to the side closer to the goal. The supporter wishes to be near enough to mark and/or tackle the ball carrier should he beat his man, yet he must be far enough away so that the dribbler cannot get by both opponents with one move.

The supporting player is positioned at an angle, a few yards to the inside of the marker. Under no circumstances can the ball carrier be allowed to take the most direct route to the goal. Therefore, the supporter is on the side of the marker that presents the most danger.

To derive the maximum benefit from having the extra player, the defensive pair must communicate. It is the supporter's responsibility to let his teammate know of his presence. This allows the marker to make an educated decision whether or not to tackle. In addition, the marker tries to force the attacker to dribble in the direction of the supporting defender.

If the defensive unit can entice its foes into a physical or mental lapse, it won't have to take risks to regain possession. One ploy is to draw the opposition into an offside position. This is an effective tool against a team that constantly "headmans" the ball (that is, passes to the attacker who is closest to the defending team's goal line).

The potential receiver tries to time his run so that the service is struck just before he breaks by the last defender. It is his objective to run onto the pass with a clear route to goal, having gotten behind the defense just after the ball was kicked forward. Reading the situation, that defender steps *past* his man just before the pass is made. Thus, when the ball is played forward, the receiver is offside.

Pulling an opponent (or opponents) offside is not always such a simple proposition. Sometimes the offense will flight a cross toward the far post for an attacker to run onto. This tactic is most often used when the ball is near the sideline and 20 to 35 yards from the goal line, with potential receivers near the edge of the far side of the penalty area.

Just before the ball can be kicked, the defensive captain (usually the keeper or the sweeper) commands his mates to run forward. The signal can be any code word imaginable, from a color to a name. It is vital that *all* defenders be near enough to the line of the attackers so that they will *all* advance past at least one opponent before the pass is struck. The failure of any defender to move expeditiously will leave the keeper to fend off an army of attackers by himself.

An automatic employment of the offside trap occurs when the ball is cleared upfield from the penalty area. The defenders move forward to force their opponents to vacate the area in front of the net.

The offside trap is a risky proposition. First, it is predicated on having competent officials. One mistake by the linesman or referee can change the outcome of the match. If a team lacks confidence in the referee, it should be wary about playing an opponent offside. Another problem is the need for the entire defense to work in concert. Many times a central defender, thinking he is the deepest of his outfield teammates, will pull up only to find that a defender on the flanks is closer to the goal line. The rule of thumb, then?

When in doubt, don't use the offside trap!

DEFENDING AGAINST DEAD-BALL PLAYS

Organization is vital when a team is confronted with defending against a dead-ball play known in soccer as a "set piece," be it a corner kick or a direct or indirect free kick. At no time is a "take-charge" goalkeeper of greater import than when having to organize a defense quickly and correctly to thwart these dangerous situations. Because the offensive team can put the ball into play as soon as it desires, the defense must react immediately.

Corner Kicks

Of all the dead-ball situations, corner kicks are the easiest to defend, because of the time it takes to retrieve the ball and the likelihood that the defending team had plenty of men behind the ball just before it left the field of play.

One defender is placed on the near goalpost while another is stationed 10 yards from the kicker and a yard or two from the goal line. The near-post defender protects against the inswinger (the curving shot on goal) since a corner is a direct kick. Should the keeper leave his line to intercept the center, that defender moves to cover the goal in case of a shot.

The defender nearest the kicker makes himself a target, hoping the ball will strike him or that his presence can harass the kicker into a subpar effort. Should the attackers place two men at the corner flag, a second defender can be added. It is his job to cover a short pass.

The goalie is positioned just in front of the back post (since it is always easier to move forward for a ball than backward). Any cross coming within six yards of the goal line and within the plane of the goalposts is his responsibility. However, if he fails to call for such a cross, the defender has no choice but to make the play himself.

A few teams opt to place a second defender on the back post. Like his colleague on the front post, he slides to cover the goal whenever the keeper leaves his line.

Not all corners will be booted directly into the goalmouth. Many teams, particularly skillful ones, like to play a "short corner." The kicker taps the ball to a teammate standing just upfield. As soon as this happens, the defender(s) on the goalposts move forward to pull the original kicker into an offside position (remember that he is only offside if the ball is played forward and he is judged to have gained an advantage by being behind the defense).

There is no excuse for the defending team not to have a numerical advantage when defending against a corner kick. *All* members of the defensive team should be between their assigned men and the goal when the ball is kicked. This includes the striker, even if he is by the midfield stripe and guarded by a pair of defenders. Failure to get goalside of all attackers allows them to ram a clearance right back into the penalty area.

Of far greater concern are free kicks awarded in and around the penalty area. In many cases, *a wall* will be needed. The more direct the angle and the closer the ball is to the goal, the more players must be used.

The number of players to be stationed in the wall is up to the keeper. He must avoid the temptation to utilize an extra player or two, or he will render his side vulnerable to a passing sequence that exploits the space behind the wall.

The wall is responsible for blocking the near side of the goal while the keeper protects the remaining part. He is also responsible for cutting out crosses lofted at an angle toward the far side.

The number of players varies with the situation. The most common range is two to six defenders (see diagram below). There are considerations beyond the position of the ball, such as the opponents' tendencies and abilities. For example, the Brazilians are famed for their incredible swerving shots. From the great Roberto Rivelino in the 1970s to Zico today, their National Team has benefited from many shots that flew above the wall before curving and dipping into the upper corner of the net.

By contrast, British teams often chip a cross toward the far side of the goal near the 6-yardline. A player runs onto the ball to either head a shot on goal or nod a service across the face of the net.

Against a team like the Brazilians, the defense can and should add an extra player in the wall and position the outer edge of the wall just past the near post to protect against a curving shot. When facing the Scots, Welsh, English, or Irish, defenders might be put to better use by manning the goalmouth.

Constructing the Wall

One outfield player is designated as the "wall captain." It is his responsibility to work in concert with the keeper to properly position this human blockade as quickly as possible.

The instant the free kick is awarded, the wall captain positions himself on

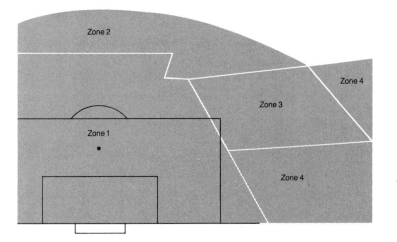

How many players should be stationed in the wall?
Zone 1: 5–6 players
Zone 2: 4 players
Zone 3: 3 players
Zone 4: 2 players

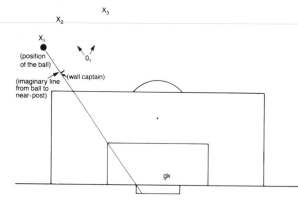

Constructing the wall. The defense's ball attacker is O1, while X2 and X3 are the offense's supporting attackers.

the imaginary direct line between the ball and the near post while facing his own net. The goalkeeper moves to the near post and directs the wall captain to be sure he is properly positioned, that is, so the outside edge of the wall bisects an imaginary line between the near post and the ball. The remaining players line up next to the wall captain, shoulder-to-shoulder, their legs together, with each player protecting his groin area with his hands.

As soon as the wall is set up (and before the opposition is ready to take the kick), the goalie positions himself halfway between the far post and the point where an imaginary line drawn from the ball to the inside of the wall would intersect with the goal line. The keeper stands a yard or two off his line (more, if he anticipates a cross to the far post; less, if he expects a dipping shot).

On a team with a stable lineup, it is possible to "number" defenders. For example, if the goalie calls for a three-man wall, the wall captain is joined by teammates number one and two.

Who should be placed in the wall? Any player who is courageous, who is likely to be in the defensive third of the field at the time of an opposition attack, and who isn't unreasonably short. Care should be taken not to place the best defensive players in the wall, since they are better used in front of the net.

Courage is vital. A ball that slips through the wall is far more dangerous than a perfectly struck shot that goes over or around it. The keeper cannot see balls kicked into the wall and has little, if any, chance to block a shot that goes through his teammates.

Many teams use deception to distract the players in the wall. Either they have one or more men run up as if to kick the ball, only to run over it, or play a square ball for a withdrawn player to strike. No matter what happens, the wall must remain intact until the ball passes by.

The square pass to a kicker who is past the inside of the wall is always a danger. The keeper must be alert, changing his angle before the shot is struck.

To protect against this offensive tactic, many teams use a "ball attacker." As soon as the initial pass is made, this kamakaze-style defender sprints to block the shot. Although he rarely touches the ball, his pressure can force the shooter

The wall. The goalkeeper and the wall captain work together to position the blockade (A). In (B), the wall, the goalie, and the ball attacker are ready. The play begins. Instead of taking a direct kick on goal, as they're entitled to do, the attacking team decides to try a square pass to an attacker beyond the range of the wall. He becomes the shooter. But the instant the ball is passed, the ball attacker sprints toward the shooter (C) at such an angle that the ball must be directed at or beyond the far post.

B   C

to mis-hit the ball. The ball attacker lines up a yard or two to the inside of the wall. He runs at the shooter from an angle that forces a shot at the far post.

Buying Time

Even more than on corners, teams need speed when defending against a free kick. A team that hesitates will find a shot headed for its net while its keeper stands yelling instructions at the near post.

There are some "tricks of the trade" that are used at higher levels of soccer to delay the taking of free kicks. While they are unsportsmanlike, not to mention illegal, they are so prevalent in professional and college ball that they are considered standard procedure and are certainly worth looking out for.

On most teams, one player will stand in front of the ball and "argue" the referee's decision. This gives his mates time to position themselves. In some cases, the player will tap the ball away (claiming that the spot of the foul was farther upfield). An accompanying tactic is for the wall to stand well within the minimum legal distance, forcing the referee to pace off 10 yards. Although the referee *should* issue yellow cards for such behavior, few do.

Nevertheless, if you're a coach, please don't teach such "tactics" to younger players. To encourage such unsportsmanlike ploys is to impart a dangerous lesson to youngsters: that winning is more important than fair play.

Goalkeeping

The soccer goalkeeper may be the only athlete in sport who considers the adjective "sure" a superior compliment to "spectacular." That's because the first-rate goalie positions himself so well and handles shots so cleanly that he rarely has to leave his feet to make the play. England's Peter Shilton probably makes fewer great saves in a month of league action than many of his counterparts make in a game—and yet he is arguably the best keeper in the world today.

This is not to say that the thrilling save made at full stretch while parallel to the ground isn't a significant weapon in the great goalkeeper's arsenal. It's just that the better keepers have to rely on it less often. They are so commanding on crosses that it is a rare occasion when they are tested on the line by a header. They cut down a shooter's angle so efficiently that the ball seems drawn to them like a magnet. They inspire such confidence in their defenders, while providing constant oral direction, that a minimum number of errors are committed in front of them. And, perhaps most important, they so deflate their opponents' confidence that simple conversions are sent sailing high or wide of the goal.

From the stands, a goalkeeper's task *appears*

103

The great goalkeepers, like New York's Hubert Birkenmeier, possess an equal measure of grace, skill, judgment, and courage.

When catching the ball, the goalkeeper's thumbs and index fingers form a "W," or "diamond," behind the ball.

relatively simple. When a ball is struck, he reacts to it. The fact is, exceptional goalkeeping demands an enormous array of physical *and* mental talent. Not only must the goalie possess great hands and be acrobatic, he must also be brave, intelligent, and a leader.

THE BASICS

Goalkeeping's first fundamental involves catching the ball. The positioning of the fingers is key.

The thumbs and index fingers combine to form a diamond behind the ball. Given the increasing power and spin of the modern player's shot, and the everpresent possibility of post-catch contact (not to mention the problems caused by wet conditions), if you're a goalkeeper, this technique must become second nature.

Known either as the "diamond" or "W," this hand positioning makes it virtually impossible for a shot to slip through. At worst, a flubbed save will find the rebound in front of, instead of precariously behind, you.

Whenever possible, you should place your hands well in advance of the anticipated point of contact with the ball. As it approaches, let your hands give slightly along the plane of the shot. This helps facilitate the "soft" hands for which great goalkeepers are famous, and which cradle the ball to safety.

The Stance

Keep your body slightly forward with your heels an inch off the ground. Bend your upper torso at the waist and position your hands above your knees and facing the shooter. Your feet should be a shoulders' width apart.

The stance. The goalie's weight is forward and evenly distributed over both feet, the center of gravity low.

Hand Position

It is always far easier to move your hands upward to meet the ball than downward. On shots that bounce in front of you, your hands should initially be positioned *below* the anticipated impact point. This provides insurance against bad hops and against shots that skid instead of bounce.

If the shot does travel in the direction anticipated, move your hands upward, bringing the ball into your chest. Your hands should be moving on the same plane as the ball.

Body Position

Because not every shot will bounce true or land on dry ground, you must try to get at least a part of your body, preferably your chest, behind the ball.

When a shot comes directly at you and is below shoulder height, you must

On shots between the shoulders and waist, the arms and chest surround the ball (left). Whenever possible, the goalkeeper tries to position his body behind the oncoming shot.

alter your catching method. Extend both arms forward as if you were being handed an infant. Surround the ball with your arms as your upper body leans forward. Doing this not only helps protect the ball, it ensures that a dropped shot will land close to you.

On shots above shoulder height, use the "W" to make the catch, and bring the ball into the chest, cradling it to safety as quickly as possible.

On ground balls, let your arms arch downward with your hands on the turf in the palms-up position. The power of the shot will propel the ball upward and into your bicep region as your hands move to surround the far side of the ball.

If time permits, you should drop to one knee with your shoulders hunched over the ball to protect against a bad bounce. On harder shots in which there isn't enough time to assume such a position, propel your shoulders forward in a straight-ahead dive as soon as your hands establish contact with the ball.

Crosses

Whenever possible, balls floated through the area should be caught cleanly at their *highest point*. Because you are the only player who can use your hands, you enjoy a 1-to-2-foot advantage over opponents. That edge is *only* applicable on balls you intercept above head height.

As with virtually all goalkeeping maneuvers, proper instantaneous judgment is vital. You must analyze where the ball will enter into your catching range and get there as it arrives. Timing is important. Arriving before the ball forces you to jump from a sedentary start, thus decreasing the altitude of your leap. Arriving too late will not only result in missing the cross, it will also leave you stranded in "no-man's-land," well out of position.

Crosses should be caught at the highest possible point.

No matter how advanced your mental attributes, there will be times when you leave the goal line to intercept a cross only to discover that you will be unable to reach the ball. Although you will be inclined to hold your ground or to retreat, do not succumb to such temptations! *Once you make your move, keep going.* By doing so you will, at least, further narrow the shooter's angle and, since he's aware of your presence, he may rush his finish and produce a sub-par shot. Fortunately, with experience, once you leave your line, you will generally intercept the cross.

After you catch the ball, bring it immediately into your chest and wrap your arms around it. Because modest jostling is as inevitable as it is difficult for the referee to detect, protecting the ball is of the uppermost importance.

Fisting Clear

There will be times in which catching a cross will either be impossible or can be executed only at the danger of dropping the ball. At such moments punching the ball to safety is your best maneuver.

As a general rule, use both hands and strike the ball in an upward motion. When punching the ball, you want to achieve, in order of priority, height, width, and distance.

Hitting the ball upward gives your defense time to recover while allowing you to return to your line. Balls fisted directly ahead or downward can ricochet into the net before you or your defense has a chance to react. Width is needed

The position of two hands when using two fists to punch the ball clear (left). The position of one hand when using one fist to punch the ball clear (right).

to put the offense out of position for a direct shot should they win possession. Distance is an added bonus. Obviously, the farther upfield the ball travels, the better. However, to punch a ball 30 yards up the center of the field is not desirable. Unless you fist the ball wide, if you're out of position you're vulnerable to a lofted shot.

Height is achieved by moving your arms upward before striking the bottom third of the ball. Width comes from following through toward the touchline. Distance results from a powerful punch in which your timing is letter-perfect.

Use of the Knee

In more advanced-level soccer, physical challenges against keepers become more prevalent. With forwards unable to reach the ball at its apex, many will employ shoulders and elbows in a manner that, while not endorsed by the laws of the game, is hard for officials to spot. With the keeper's arms extended, his chest and stomach are vulnerable targets for the forward, who—let's face it—includes intimidation among his tactics.

To protect yourself against such challenges, leap off one leg while lifting your opposite knee in front of you. Although it is illegal to employ that knee as a weapon, most referees will condone its use as long as you use it defensively.

ANGLE PLAY

The ability to narrow an attacker's shooting angle is what allows the exceptional keeper to leave his feet less often. In most instances, taking a few steps toward the shooter markedly decreases his target area.

There are three basic "zones" (see diagram) you can use as a goalie to analyze where to position yourself. When an opponent is unmarked in front of the goal (labeled "zone one"), expect a direct shot, and, as a rule, move out near the 6 yardline. Remember, you want to cut down the shooter's target area. In stepping forward, time your movement so that your feet are set as the opponent shoots.

Be careful not to come out too far or you will increase your vulnerability to the lofted shot or to a pass across the goalmouth. Unless an opponent breaks completely free of all potential markers, you should not advance past the 6 yardline.

Shots from "zone two" present less of a problem. Whereas a shot from

Good goalies leave their feet less often because they are so adept at narrowing a shooter's angle. By moving just a few yards forward from the goal line, the goalkeeper lessens the distance he must cover to intercept a shot aimed just inside either post.

The three major shooting zones.

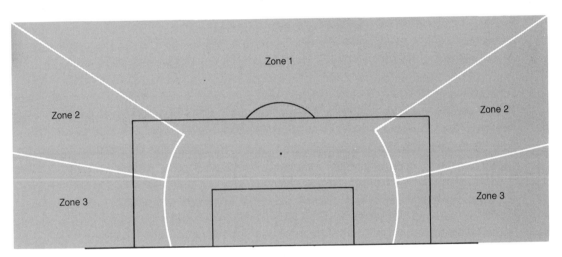

"zone one" can be struck to either post, a ball from beyond the plane of the goalpost requires exceptional accuracy and pace to be successful. Because of that, the skillful forward's best scoring chance comes if you misposition yourself. By excessively cutting down the angle, you are exposed to the chipped shot. The more acute the shooter's angle, the closer you should be to your line.

"Zone three" is the "crossing zone." As long as a defender on your team is positioned between the ball carrier and the goal, your opponent's best option is the centering pass. In this case, retreat toward the far post while staying close to the goal line. Because it is always easier to move forward than to backpedal, you must be concerned with keeping the play in front of you. However, should the forward break free on the flank or back your defender toward the net, you

A   B

The full-stretch diving save. In this sequence, David Brcic shows the form that has made him one of the greatest American-born goalies in soccer history. The Cosmos star pushes off his inside foot after lifting his opposite leg to add momentum to his dive (A).

must move toward the ball. This protects against a quick pass to a rival on the strong side or a direct shot toward the near post.

One point to remember is that if the ball is rolling *away* from the shooter, it will be very difficult for him to chip a shot delicately over you and under the bar. This allows you the luxury of taking an extra yard to further decrease the shooter's angle.

Conversely, a ball rolling toward the kicker, or one that is under his control, is a danger signal, saying *Be wary of the lofted shot.*

Consider, too, the distance of any shot. The closer the shooter is to the goal, the closer you as keeper want to be to the ball when it is struck.

Shooters moving onto a ball as they run across the field will find it difficult to kick the ball with power toward the direction from which they came.

DIVING AND JUMPING

Sometimes shots on goal will be so far away from you and moving so fast, that you must leave your feet to make the save. Diving techniques vary with the type and location of the shot. The most common dive involves full body extension in order to intercept a shot in midair. As the shot comes your way, your outer foot (i.e., your left foot when diving to your right) leaves the ground first with the bent knee moving upward and across your body. By doing so, you've initiated thrust so that your body weight shifts in the direction you will dive. At that point, your near-sided foot pushes off the ground to propel you toward the ball.

When making the catch, once again, forefingers and thumbs form the diamond. As soon as you establish control of the shot, your hands should turn *toward* the field of play so that they are on top of the ball in the ten o'clock

He then reaches to make the catch, keeping his eyes on the ball while his hands form the "W" (B). As David lands, the ball strikes the ground *first*, with his hands on top of it (C). David then draws the ball against his body (D).

and two o'clock positions. This is extremely important since the correct completion of this dive requires that the ball hit the ground *before* the body! Why? The ball cushions your fall, and also prevents you from striking your "funny bone" against the turf, which could result in yielding a rebound.

Difficult as it may seem, always land on your side after a diving save. Under no circumstance should your body turn. Any goalie who lands on his stomach or uses his hands to break his fall will only magnify the impact, not lessen it.

The Grounder

You'll find yourself using still another type of diving save when stopping shots on the turf. Both the leg thrust and the hand motion you'll need differ from other dives, and the proper execution of both is extremely important since a rebound on this type of save leaves you lying on the ground while the ball rolls a few feet in front of an unprotected goal. Indeed, yielding rebounds is just about *the* most fatal error a goalkeeper can make.

To make a diving save of a ground-level shot, your near hand (that is, your right hand when diving to the right) sweeps along the ground with the thumb and index finger extended upward to form the bottom half of the diamond. The

When saving a ground-level shot, the hands lead the body into the dive, with the near-sided hand *behind* the ball.

upper (far-sided) hand comes over the top of the ball. On impact, both the thumb and index finger of the upper hand are slightly to the back side of the ball.

Why not let the hands move sideways in concert? Simple. The ball might take a bad bounce. Because the penalty area sees a disproportionate amount of action, it is usually the first segment of the field to lose its grass and evenness, so tricky hops are an unhappy fact of life with which all goalkeepers must cope. With your upper hand positioned above shoulder height, you are able to parry the bad bounce shot out of danger *even* if that hop occurs *after* you are into your dive. With your upper hand above your shoulder and moving toward the ball, you can still deflect the bad hop toward the least dangerous rebound position. Had your hand been underneath the flight of the ball, the rebound would deflect straight upward where any opponent could score with a simple touch-in. Furthermore, any shot with considerable spin can be handled more easily with two hands moving from different directions to trap the ball against the turf.

When diving to save a grounder, your leg thrust must be outward off the side of the foot, *not* upward. Again, the near-sided foot propels the body, leaving the ground after your far knee has begun to move upward and to the side.

On shots within the length of your outstretched body, let your near leg collapse underneath you. On ground dives, your hands lead the way, and always with your near-sided hand as close to ground level as possible throughout the duration of the dive.

Sometimes it isn't possible to reach the ball with both hands. In (A), University of Vermont All-American Skip Gilbert guides the ball around the post, using his palm. In (B), the ball arrives *above* the plane of Skip's body, so he rotates his body in midair and uses his far-side hand to deflect the shot around the post.

A   B

The Full-Stretch Save

When *every inch* counts on the dive, use only your near-sided hand and let your open palm guide the ball around the near post. There is one exception to this rule. On high shots above the plane of the body, use your far-sided hand. On this type of save your upper body rotates in midair with your far hand coming over the top. As it does, the outside of the hand is above and slightly behind the thumb, and your palm pushes the ball out of danger.

Over-the-Top Parry

Another variety of parry save involves directing shots over the crossbar. Used whenever a high ball cannot be caught cleanly, this maneuver utilizes both hands palming the shot in an upward motion. On more powerful shots, you may need only one hand.

On rising shots you merely redirect the ball; the pace of the shot will carry it to safety. On a dipping chip shot, you push up firmly at such an angle that the ball clears the bar. Because a palm provides a greater striking surface than a fist, use the open hand on *all* rising shots and on most sinking ones. The one exception comes when you are trying to save a dipping ball some distance from the goal line. In this case, you want to strike the ball hard enough so that it will not land behind you within the field of play. In this case *only,* a clenched fist is acceptable. Using a fist otherwise risks having the ball skim off your knuckles without them having adequately altered the ball's line of flight.

The position of the palm for deflecting a shot over the crossbar (left). In the action shot from the 1982 World Cup (right), the goalie redirects a cross over the bar. Note how his body faces the direction from which the ball was struck.

Saving the Chip Shot

When saving a lofted shot, such as a chip shot, you'll often find you must retreat prior to your leap. If the ball is high and close to the goal, use your fingertips to redirect it over the crossbar. Under no circumstances while backpedaling should you ever turn your body sideways or cross your feet.

JUDGMENT

When in doubt while playing goal, you should *always opt for safety.* The worst thing you can do is to attempt a catch only to drop the ball in the goalmouth. Unless you are fully confident that you can hold the ball, you should play it safe and fist or palm the ball out of danger.

Make no mistake: You should catch whatever you can. Continually redirecting catchable balls subjects your defense to unnecessary pressure, which can make it more prone to committing panic-ridden mistakes. Surehandedness, decisiveness, making the right kind of save—these are the things that inspire the confidence that every good backline needs to have in its goalkeeper.

LEADERSHIP

Speaking Up

There is another important muscle you should always use whenever you leave your line to intercept a cross: your vocal cords! It's hard enough battling opponents for a cross without having to climb a defender's back first. Since you are the *only* player who can see the entire play developing in front of you, as you vacate the goalmouth, it is your responsibility to make sure your teammates are aware that you are moving. This allows your defenders to get out of your way. A defender who does not have a specific opponent to mark should retreat to guard the area you vacated just in case an opponent should beat you to the ball.

Make your call consistent—and never yell "Mine." Any player could say that. When you want the ball, scream "Keeper" so authoritatively that players on both benches scramble to get out of the way! And don't worry about the offense yelling that same signal near your goal. By the laws of soccer, any opponent that tries to trick the defense by yelling "Keeper" is guilty of ungentlemanly conduct. The referee should award an indirect free kick, and may issue a yellow card.

Communication is another leadership function in goalkeeping. A keeper who fails to help out his defense by providing direction and guidance has no one but himself to blame when an unmarked forward scores.

The good goalie doesn't watch the ball all the time. There are instances when you can "steal a glance" to analyze what is occurring away from the point of attack. For example, if the opposition is advancing the ball up the right side, you should quickly look to your left to ascertain if all opponents are marked. Often the defense will pinch toward the ball, leaving the offense's far-sided winger or midfielder dangerously free.

The best time to take your eyes off the ball is when the player in possession will need an extra touch (or more) before crossing the ball (such as when he is trying to dribble around a defender or has the ball on his inside foot).

Sometimes your team may be caught on a quick counterattack and find itself outnumbered. When this happens, you should instruct your weak-side defender(s) to take up a central position so each defender can move to any one of a few opponents in no more time than it would take to pass him the ball. You must also analyze which of your teammates currently upfield will be able to recover the quickest to assume a helpful defensive posture. You should instruct those men to pick up opponents *away* from the ball while those already in good defensive locations attempt to slow down the attack.

Another ingredient you must analyze is defensive support. Always instruct your teammate marking the opponent in possession as to whether he is in a one-on-one situation, or whether there are extra defenders in supporting positions. This allows the marker to make an educated decision concerning the prudence of an immediate challenge versus jockeying his opponent to buy time.

Viewing, as I do every year, more than a hundred soccer matches at all levels, I'm astonished at how often communications between a goalie and his defense are neglected. They shouldn't be. Many times a team will leave their goalie virtually defenseless by failing to mark opponents properly. Fans and coaches alike tend to dismiss the resulting goal as "not the keeper's fault." But when the goalie fails to inform his defenders of dangerous situations that are unfolding out of their line of sight, the resulting breakdown and score are, indeed, the goalie's fault.

LOOSE-BALL PLAY

The least favorite activity of most goalkeepers is diving into an opponent's feet for a loose ball. It's a skill that requires timing, quickness, and a lot of (pick

Courage is a prerequisite between the posts. In Soccer Bowl–82, Seattle's Paul Hammond fearlessly slides his upper body across the face of the goal and into the ball's path just as the ball is kicked by Rick Davis.

one) courage or stupidity. The conscientious goalie is willing, even anxious, to do whatever is needed to make the play.

If you can get to the loose ball first, you have an option. You can dive on top of the ball or you can scoop it up on the run.

When opting for the former, use your upper body to cover the ball. This can be a discomforting experience but it is necessary, since failure to do so can result in the tricky forward kicking the ball out of your hands when the referee's view is blocked.

Should you get to the ball a full stride (or more) ahead of your rival *and* should the ball be off the ground, you can pick it up without breaking stride. Do this keeping your shoulders forward and over the ball. Your arms wrap around the ball and bring it immediately into the upper body. Your body's momentum causes the weight to be shifted forward.

As the opponent arrives, jump over his feet and land with your arms tightly cradling the ball.

The 50-50 Ball

Sometimes you'll find yourself racing an opponent for a 50-50 ball that is rolling away from the offensive player and toward you. To make the save, you must slide *before* your opponent can touch the ball, keeping your body perpendicular to the incoming opponent's path. In this way, your body blocks the face of the goal. Concentrate all your attention on the ball, taking it in front of the *upper* part of your torso.

Once again, you've got to have courage. An opponent bent on intimidation can take an "inaccurate" kick "at" the ball, only to strike you "instead." Although you may appear to be defenseless against such ruthless tactics, such is not the case. By sliding *at an angle* in which your feet slightly precede your body, your knees can be tucked to protect the rest of you. In fact, some advanced-level goalkeepers bent on intimidation themselves will often expose their cleats toward an opponent's oncoming shins. This technique has no place in youth soccer circles, and should have no place in soccer at any level. The sorry fact of life, however, is that older players should be aware of various means of self-defense against overly aggressive foes.

Breakaways

Another loose-ball situation you can expect as a goalie, is one in which the forward gains possession first. If he has a good shooting angle and has gotten past (behind) the final defender, you must dive into his feet. Your actions are dictated by how quickly you can get to the forward's shooting foot at the instant he gains control. If the distance exceeds a couple of yards, you must advance rapidly while keeping your hands low to the ground. The faster the ball and opponent are moving, the more difficult it will be for the shooter to lift the ball over you and yet under the crossbar. Be prepared to hit the ground on this play. As you advance, turn the palms of your hands toward the shooter. (It is important to move rapidly *but not out of control,* lest the skillful rival dribble around you.) Then, as the play unfolds, keep your eyes fixed on the ball. (It is a sin to be beaten by a shoulder or hip fake!)

Many times the attacker will get to the ball just before you do. When this happens, you must slide into your foe's legs *before* the ball can be shot. Using the upper body to block as much of the goal as possible, make yourself into as big a target as you can so that the ball cannot help but strike your body.

Of all the tasks goalkeepers must perform, this one requires the most intestinal fortitude by far. You must be willing to absorb the brunt of a 70-mile-per-hour shot that was struck a few feet away without care as to where the ball might impact. Your hands are extended *past* your head. This is done to block more of the goal while preventing your opponent from dribbling around that side. Thus, yes, your face, as well as your body, is exposed.

Many a keeper, including a surprising number of professionals, will throw their feet at the ball. While this technique may be endorsed by dentists and the folks at Blue Cross, it increases the opponent's chance of scoring. Although all keepers hate having to save the breakaway shot, it comes with the territory.

Acute-Angle Breakaways

No matter how little time you have to prepare yourself against a breakaway, you should always make note of the *direction* from which the offensive player is approaching. The more acute his angle, the more likely he'll try to dribble around you. Under that circumstance, you must try to force your opponent toward the goal line *on the short side* (away from the center of the field). You can do this by modifying the angle of your approaching run so that the shooter sees more space on the near-post side. This "exposed" side you'll cover using your upper body and arms. By overplaying the far side, you force the ball carrier to go in the direction that you prefer. Additionally, if the attacker is able to get around you, he must strike a shot from a tough angle while running full speed away from his target.

Should this goalie-attacker confrontation occur close to the goal line, it may not be necessary for you to touch the ball in order to prevent a score. Merely by forcing the attacker to change direction sharply at full speed, you may cause him to lose control of the ball. Think of the goal line as your ally, robbing the offensive player of desperately needed space.

In *all* one-on-one situations, your hands must be positioned as close to the turf as possible. The faster the attacker is moving, the more likely the shot will be on the ground. Most airborne shots will sail harmlessly over the bar (since they must go almost straight up to clear your body, which is within a few feet of the shooter's foot as the ball is kicked). Even if an airborne shot is on target, it is always far easier to move your hands (or even a foot) upward to make the play than it is to move them downward. A mere touch of the ball will force it over the crossbar when the shot is rising.

You'll find that on most point-blank saves, catching the ball cleanly is an impossibility. Try to do the next best thing, which is to deflect the ball as far away from danger as you can. For most shots, you can accomplish this by angling your palm outward to parry the ball wide.

OVERCOMING PHYSICAL SHORTCOMINGS

All keepers want, whenever possible, to handle shots cleanly. Unfortunately, only a handful of people who play the position possess the physical attributes to do this almost all the time. Like many of my colleagues, I have relatively small hands. The full-stretch diving save that a Jan van Beveren makes with ease would result in a disastrous drop in the goalmouth if attempted by a Dan Herbst. You too? Don't fret. Like me, and thousands of other goalkeepers, you may have to modify the *ideal* technique that all goalkeepers are taught, to best suit your individual strengths and weaknesses. Even on the professional level, there are plenty of goalies who are "too short" or "too tall," "too slow" or "too light," and/or otherwise "handicapped."

If you're a short goalie, you may need to rely heavily on quickness to survive. Short goalies tend not to cut down the shooter's angle as much so as to protect against the chip shot (which, obviously, gives them more difficulty than it does their taller counterparts). As a short goalie you should possess enough quickness to get to most shots on the line (especially low ones).

On the other hand, if you're a big, hulking specimen, as a rule you probably *will* have troubles on the line, since you're far less likely to be able to match a smaller colleague's quickness or acrobatic ability. Again, no reason to fret: By slightly overplaying your angles and coming out to challenge the shooter, you make yourself such a big target that your slower reflexes are rarely exposed.

When I played goal, I always tried to minimize the deficiencies of my less-than-perfect hands by encouraging the opponent to shoot where I wanted him to. I used this tactic anytime a foe had an angled shot from within the penalty area.

What I feared was a ball well struck toward the far post. If I was to parry such a shot, the rebound would roll dangerously in front of an unprotected net. It was my wish, then, that the shooter aim for the near side, which allowed me to make the save *and* deflect the ball over the goal line, thereby yielding only a corner kick.

To encourage the near-post shot, I intentionally "misplayed" my angle away from that side. The shooter would perceive a near-side opening that was, in reality, a mirage. Why a mirage? Because what he didn't notice was that my weight had shifted so that I was leaning toward the short side (and thus was able to dive in that direction more quickly). I always calculated the shooter's power, the distance of the shot, the acuteness of the angle, my own quickness, and the distance between where I was standing and where I would have to reach in order to protect the entire near side (which was *never* more than could be covered with a full-stretch dive). I was careful never to violate goalkeeping's first tenet: "Don't ever get beat to the short side."

None of this, of course, had appeared in any goalkeeping manual that I had ever seen. Quite the opposite. As a rule, the near post is zealously guarded. Most keepers would prefer a shot toward the far side since the ball must travel a greater distance and thus 1) is more likely to be blocked by a central defender and 2) allows the keeper more time to react.

Trouble is, this rule applies to all goalies *except* those of us whose physical tools are not best designed for such shots. By knowing your limitations as well as your assets, you can devise ways of minimizing your personal deficiencies.

This ability to think for yourself is critical if you are to reach your maximum potential as a goalkeeper. If you're a young player, by all means watch the pros, learn from them, and perhaps even pattern yourself after your hero. But be aware, too, that you may not be blessed with the same physical gifts as an Alan Mayer or a Shep Messing. Still, though, if you can outthink your opponent, you need not necessarily be physically superior in order to beat him.

PENALTY KICKS

Just how tough is it for a goalie to save a penalty kick? Consider that the hapless keeper is granted roughly two-tenths of one second to stop a 70 mph shot aimed at a 192-square-foot target from 12 yards out.

Needless to say, it is virtually impossible for a keeper to react to a properly taken penalty and make the block. All you can do is guess which way the shot will go and dive accordingly. *If* you guess right, *if* the ball isn't shot well, and *if* you hit your dive perfectly, you *may* get lucky and make the save. The higher the caliber of play, the less likely that your goals-against-average will survive a penalty kick unscathed. Nevertheless, here are techniques for improving your chances of a save against this kick.

1) Make your initial movement forward, *not* to the side. If you are fortunate enough to touch the ball, you want to be at least a yard off your line so you can parry the shot around the post instead of back into play. To move forward, leap toward the shooter, landing on the balls of your feet.

2) As soon as your feet touch the ground, use your legs to propel you sideways in the direction you think the shot will come. Most well-struck penalties will travel close to the ground, so the dive should accentuate distance, not altitude.

There are certain tricks that you can legally use in such confrontations. For example, as the kicker approaches the ball, you can sway in the direction opposite in which you intend to dive, throwing your elbow outward in an exaggerated movement. If the shooter planned to place the ball toward the side of the feint, he may be persuaded to add pace to his shot or to aim closer to the post. Either could cause a miss. Ideally, the shooter will commit the cardinal sin of changing his mind at the final instant, the number one cause of botched kicks.

Keep in mind, you have virtually no chance of making the save if the kicker performs his task correctly. Your greatest hope lies in inducing a subpar effort from your foe. If you're presently playing youth or high-school soccer, you might be better advised to trust your reflexes. As the kick is taken, leap forward with your hands held outside the plane of the body. Your body weight is evenly distributed with the knees slightly bent so as to obtain maximum power and distance on the subsequent dive to the side.

Still, no matter if you are playing in an AYSO match or the NASL, you should know the rules governing the penalty kick. The shooter first of all must be clearly identified and is the only other player besides the goalie allowed inside the penalty area, or arc, prior to the shot. He cannot take the kick until the referee blows his whistle. The shot must be taken in one continuous motion. It is illegal for the shooter to pause before kicking in order to ascertain where the keeper will dive. Should any of these regulations be violated by the kicker or by a member of the opposing team, and the ball goes in the net, the kick must be retaken.

On the other hand, should the goalie be judged to have moved prematurely (or if parts of both feet were not in contact with the goal line as the ball was shot) or if a defensive player entered the penalty area or arc before the shot, the kick will be retaken should the shooter have failed to score.

If the shot ricochets off the goalpost *without* being touched by the keeper, the kicker cannot play the ball until someone else does first. Should the shooter touch the ball directly after a rebound, the defending team is awarded an indirect free kick from the spot of the second touch.

DISTRIBUTION

Contrary to what some people choose to believe, your goalkeeping chores are not completed when you make a save. Just as you are the last player on defense, you are the first man on offense. What you do with the ball after you've gained possession can mark the difference between a successful counterattack and an errant clearance that is intercepted, thus exposing your defense to further pressure.

Distribution includes punting, drop kicking, throwing, and rolling the ball. It also means having the skill to take your own goal kicks (why waste a defender, thus having one less potential receiver?).

Selecting the best means of release involves several variables including the specific game situation (such as the score, time remaining, and placement of players) as well as weather and field conditions, the ability of your teammates, and the size of the field.

Each means of distribution boasts unique qualities to recommend its usage.

A throw is the quickest and most accurate way of getting the ball to a teammate, while a punt covers the most ground. The drop kick can travel farther than the throw while delivering greater accuracy than a punt. And the roll is the easiest for the receiver to control on the first touch. Which to choose?

Many coaches will instruct their goalie always to use a specific form of distribution. Most often at the scholastic and youth levels, punting is in vogue. On teams with limited skill, this is a solid tactical approach. It allows the defense to clear the ball upfield without risking a turnover in its own half of the field.

Unfortunately, it demands a price. Defenders on a team that never builds up play from the rear will find they retard their progress in developing good close control and skill in tight quarters. In addition, the keeper will never develop the ability to make the proper decision as to where and how to distribute the ball in different situations. These are aspects of the game that players will need to have mastered as they progress to more advanced levels. Thus, "playing to win" at the grass-roots level is not always compatible with teaching the game properly.

Throwing

Not surprisingly, throwing is the skill that most North Americans find easiest to master. With our sports background usually including at least some baseball, basketball, and/or football experience, we have a basic understanding of how to toss a ball.

The soccer goalie uses three forms of throwing:

The Baseball Throw
The baseball throw involves an overhead delivery in which you bend your elbow. Position your hand behind the ball and propel it first by bringing the

The baseball throw. The elbow of the throwing arm is slightly bent and the shoulders are perpendicular to the target.

When rolling the ball to a teammate, make your release when your arm is perpendicular to the ground.

arm back to a point where the ball is to the side of the ear and then forward and down, with the ball released at the apex of the motion. Use the baseball throw for medium-distance tosses.

The Roll

As its name implies, the roll is an underhanded service in which the ball travels along the ground to its intended target. Limited to distributions of fairly modest distances it can be easily controlled by the receiver.

The technique for the soccer roll is nearly identical with that used by a bowler. Cup the underside of the ball with your throwing hand and swing your arm back to waist height, all the while keeping your hand under the ball. As the downswing begins, step forward with your opposite foot and point it toward the target. Release the ball while the arm is perpendicular to the ground.

The Overhead Throw

This third variety of throw combines the motions of discus and javelin throwing.

Position your body sideways to your intended receiver, with your non-throwing shoulder closer to the target. Your throwing hand should be behind the ball, cupping it against your wrist. Lower your throwing shoulder so that your arm can reach back to hip height. Your arm swing should then come straight over the top, passing to the side of the head. Throughout the entire process your elbow never bends. You release the ball just after your arm is overhead, in line with your body.

The overhead, or javelin, throw. Keep the ball cupped against the wrist and the shoulders parallel to the target during the backswing.

Of all the throws, the overhead can be delivered with the greatest pace and distance. You'll find it most useful when you intercept a cross and wish to exploit the opportunity for a quick counter.

Options

As a rule, unless you distribute the ball within a second of catching it, it is best to wait a considerable time before releasing it.

Rolling

Generally, roll the ball only after the opposition has retreated upfield. Advanced players follow this rule since a defending team knows the chances of a turnover are slim and does not, therefore, wish to spread itself too thin (it is easier for eleven men to cover half a field than an entire one, since there is less space for the attackers to utilize).

If the other team decides to apply pressure after a save or if your teammates lack advanced skill, rolling the ball entails risks. However, if the skill level of your teammates is sufficient to withstand challenges, rolling is a good way not to risk losing possession on the distribution (as opposed to a punt, which is a fifty-fifty proposition). Also, keep in mind, if there are no opponents behind your receiver, he can always play the ball back to you should he be challenged.*

*As of press time, FIFA was contemplating a rule to outlaw such back passing. It is advisable to check the current laws of the game on this matter.

Punting

Another option after a save is to punt the ball. When doing this you should allow *all* of your teammates to advance to the midfield area. This will force opponents to vacate their offensive section of the field so as to avoid being in an offside position should one of their players win the ball and play it forward.

The smaller the field's dimensions, the better weapon a punt becomes. A narrow field decreases space for an interpassing buildup (thus making the advancement of the ball through a series of short passes more vulnerable to an interception). The shorter the field, the closer the punt will land to the other team's goal.

The technique for punting is relatively simple. Hold the ball in both hands with your palms facing upward, your fingers slightly below the height of the palm. Drop the ball in front of your body as your kicking foot moves to strike it.

Sometimes a keeper will fail to strike the ball on the surface of his shoelaces (instep); instead, the ball lands on the shin pads or the edge of the toes. Dropping the ball incorrectly is usually the source of this mistake.

Release the ball so that you *must step forward* to kick. Dropping the ball too close to the body inhibits the leg swing, resulting in an unacceptable ratio of altitude to distance, while dropping the ball too far ahead will produce a punt that is dangerously low and short.

To obtain maximum power, your shoulders should be forward at the time of the drop and your body should be bent slightly at the waist.

Many European and South American goalkeepers can punt proficiently with either foot. This skill is most valuable since it allows them to launch a good kick even when an opponent (who must be stationary) is blocking the path to their "good" foot.

Drop Kicking

The drop kick is the toughest distribution-related skill that most Americans encounter. As the name implies, the ball is dropped to the ground and volleyed as soon as it bounces. The body leans well forward so the instep can drive through the ball.

Lower and more accurate than a punt, the drop kick is ideal when you are kicking into a strong wind. However, an uneven or ill-kept field can create bad bounces and cause a mis-kick. Wet fields can also be a hazard. Should your planting foot slip on wet ground, the ball could roll right to an opponent while you lie helplessly on your back.

Nevertheless, a well-struck drop kick is a great *offensive* weapon since it

The drop kick. David strikes the ball just after it has bounced and as his weight shifts forward.

can cover a great distance quickly. It can reach an open teammate in the attacking portion of the field so fast that he has time and space to exploit after receiving the ball, and, when quickly taken, a drop kick can often catch the opposition napping.

Decision-Making

Distribution selection is also influenced by the scoreboard. If your team is nursing a lead in the waning moments of a game, you might be best advised to take an extra moment before returning the ball into play. The same holds true after your goal has been under siege. By taking your time, you give your team time to catch their collective breath and regroup.

You must take great care never to lose the ball on a distribution within your own half of the field. To do so is to invite trouble. Inevitably, when you gain possession, your teammates begin thinking offensively. Defenders who have specific marking assignments will have left their men to free themselves for a pass. The fullbacks move wide while midfielders run into space. Thus, if your pass is picked off, the other team's most dangerous players will be wide open in the attacking third of the park.

When in doubt, hold the ball and wait before distributing it. Never, ever, throw the ball to a teammate in traffic. Never pass to a receiver who has his back to the opponent's goal *unless* the receiver has adequate support in the direction that he is facing or is so wide open that he will have plenty of room in which to turn after the ball arrives.

The key word here is "pass." Like any service, a keeper's throw should, if possible, bounce in front of the receiver, so it can be easily controlled.

According to the laws of the game, you are allowed to take only four steps with the ball in your possession. If a violation is spotted, the other team will be awarded an indirect free kick from the spot of the extra step.

Where to Look

Because the quick pass to an open player is the most effective means of distribution, it is imperative that you know where to look first. Invariably, you'll find the most open space on the *opposite* side of the field from which the ball came. Thus, if a cross, shot, or back pass to you originates from your right side, you should immediately look to your far left. Even at the most advanced levels of soccer, players tend to be attracted to the ball and funnel toward the goal. By looking in the opposite direction right away, you will not only find an open teammate (most likely), you'll also punish any opponents whose transition game is a trifle slow. This is especially true when you win the ball in the air as opposed to saving it on the line or after a back pass from a teammate.

Back-Passing to the Keeper

Passing back to one's own goalie is a simple solution to often sticky defensive situations. Nevertheless, it is a play on which far too many inexcusable errors are made.

If a teammate has his back to the opponent's net and does not have room in which to turn, and if the path to your goal is not trespassed by an opposition player, you should forcefully call for the ball. The defender then should *immediately* pass the ball back to you, striking it with power in a direction just outside the near post. Good pace on the pass will assure that an opponent won't beat you to the ball. And aiming wide of the near post ensures that, if you do miss the pass, your error won't result in an embarrassing goal. To put it another way, it is far better to let the ball roll out of bounds and yield five corner kicks than it is to risk kicking the ball into one's own net. The defender should run toward you after passing, shielding his rival until he is sure you will get to the ball first. At that point he moves upfield and toward the sideline to be open for a pass from you.

READING THE GAME

This is another aspect of goalkeeping in which your leadership and judgment come into play. You must constantly note the position of the ball, your teammates, and opponents, in order to best provide positive vocal support and guidance. Your ability to sense danger and alert your mates can play as big a part in maintaining a good goals-against-average as the dramatic diving save. Known as "reading the game," this ability is what separates exceptional from average goalies.

The outstanding goalie takes nothing for granted. San Diego Sockers star Alan Mayer, considered by many to be the finest native North American goalkeeper of all time, suggests that keepers "always be prepared. Never expect that your defenders will play an error-free game. A goalie must always anticipate possible mistakes so that he is ready when one is made."

Reading the game also involves analyzing the opposition. When the action is in the other half of the field, the alert goalkeeper becomes a scout. He discovers which opponents have a favorite foot and who relies more on power than finesse. That knowledge can prove invaluable when the keeper faces that rival in a one-on-one confrontation.

Also worth noting is the overall style of the rival team. Are their passing skills polished or do they employ a "kick-and-run" approach? Most experienced keepers love facing the latter. Because kick-and-run soccer teams usually lack refined passing skill, you should not hesitate to take liberties when cutting down the shooting angle of a player on such a team. You'll find, too, when playing against the kick-and-run game, that with many balls being booted aimlessly upfield, you'll be serving as a second sweeper. When the ball is in the opponents' half of the field, move to the top of your own penalty area, and be ready to win any stray through balls. With your hand-use limited to the 44-by-18-yard penalty area, your kicking skills will be put to the test.

Many keepers like to leave the goalmouth whenever the ball is out of range. This allows them to be closer to the game. They can spy openings better and call out instructions to teammates. Doing this not only helps make their teammates' jobs easier, it also keeps the goalie mentally alert.

This is more important than it sounds. A real danger is the temporary loss of concentration when the play is upfield for any length of time. Just because the ball is 70 yards away doesn't mean you have license to relax. To relax is to run the risk of yielding a cheap goal, an occurrence that can be devastating to a team's morale. Whatever devices you need to employ, you must remain mentally alert at all times.

One player I know went so far as to "announce" the game just as a play-by-play television reporter would. While his method was a bit unusual, it worked for him, and that's all that matters. Of equal import, he had all the skills of an accomplished outfield player. If he needed to head a ball from danger, he could do it consistently. It didn't matter where the ball was since he was two-footed.

His skill was no accident. As a youngster he had spent considerable time playing other positions. Occasionally in intrasquad scrimmages he would play in the midfield.

All goalkeepers should possess the skill to play outside their penalty area when needed and be capable of taking their own goal kicks. Stated simply: *Just because a goalkeeper is the only player who can use his hands doesn't mean he has to be the only one who can't use his feet!*

Set Pieces

Dead-ball situations—those in which a team is awarded a free kick or a corner kick—can present a great scoring opportunity to a team that is well prepared, skillful, and intelligent enough to capitalize on the advantage. When faced with a dead-ball situation (better known in soccer as a set piece) such as a free kick, a team can either immediately attempt a shot on goal on the first or second touch or work a predesigned passing sequence in hope of attaining a better scoring opportunity. Which option your team should employ depends on a number of factors.

The most important considerations are the location of the ball, the positioning of the defenders, and the skill of your own team. Obviously, you will be more inclined to attempt a direct shot on net when awarded a free kick at the top of the penalty area than when you are awarded one from the side of the box. By shooting on the first or second touch, your offense does not risk having to execute any difficult passes and your team can be sure that your best finisher will take the shot. You must also take into consideration the defense's alignment. If the opposition has committed too many players to the wall, there may be a large gap *behind* the wall that your team can exploit. If the

131

Dead-ball plays—better known in soccer as "set pieces"—provide an excellent scoring opportunity *if* an attacking team is well prepared.

wall lines up incorrectly, leaving room to shoot inside the near post, a direct shot from a seemingly bad angle becomes inviting. The third ingredient in the decision-making process involves your offense's attacking ability. If your team is one blessed with many gifted athletes, you may use an involved passing sequence to obtain a better finishing opportunity than would be presented by a first- or second-touch shot. Masters at intricate pass combinations were the Dutch National Teams of the 1974 and 1978 World Cups.

Because the defense has time to set up, the goalmouth is likely to be well protected. When using this approach, the objective is to get a close-in shot from directly in front of the net.

BASIC SET PLAYS

Deception is the key ingredient in making a set play successful. The more players the opposition has in its wall and the farther that wall is from the goal line, the better the opportunity to exploit the space behind it.

For example, if the defense has committed five men to its wall, it will only have five outfield players with which to defend the goalmouth. What the team on attack hopes to do is induce those defenders to abandon that territory. The attackers can do this in two ways: 1) The ball can be played *around* the box. At least one defender must come to mark the ball carrier and others are likely to "ball-watch," thus making it easier for attackers off the ball to get open. 2) The attacking team can have players in the goalmouth run *away* from the net. This will bring markers with them, allowing a withdrawn attacker to exploit the space that their movement creates.

By using the field's width, the offensive team pulls defenders toward the ball and, therefore, away from the precious turf in front of the net. As defenders come to the ball, attackers make intelligent runs *behind* their markers. A cross

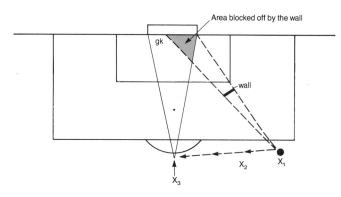

Basic set play: a square ball followed by a shot on goal. This is an excellent play to use when an attacking team wins a free kick at an angle from the goalmouth. As shown here, the defense's wall, at such an angle, leaves X1 (the player on the ball) with only half the goal to shoot for, so he passes a square ball to his teammate, X3, who takes the clearer shot. Since no defender can be within 10 yards of the ball until the first touch, X3 is hard to mark. Only if he strays more than 10 yards from the ball can a marker cover him before the ball is put into play.

to the far-post area should find an open attacker (see diagram page 75 right).

A slightly more complicated choice is to chip a cross just past the far post. As the defense turns to face the ball it will invariably overcompensate, moving toward the ball and leaving gaps behind it and at the top of the penalty area. A player at the far-post heads the ball toward the penalty spot. A withdrawn player can run onto the ball as it is headed backward for a direct shot on goal.

THE SET-UP

As the attacking team lines up, it should have at least three players in position for a first- or second-touch shot on goal, regardless of whether it is a direct or indirect free kick. Of these, two players should be near the ball, with the third slightly behind the ball and just past the inside plane of the wall.

The most basic play involves a square pass for the third offensive man to run onto for a shot. Because of his angle of approach, he will have the whole net to shoot for, thus negating the effectiveness of the wall.

Even if the offense plans to use a passing sequence, this basic alignment still forces the opposition to defend against the first- or second-touch shot!

Another possibility is for the first man who approaches the ball to feign a shot and run over the ball. He can then move into open space or run at the keeper to distract the goalie's concentration on the ball. The second player either shoots or puts into motion a prearranged passing sequence. By having one man run over the ball, the offensive team hopes either to "freeze" defenders, cause defenders to ball-watch, or induce a player in the wall to move, leaving a hole that the shooter can place the ball through. Another advantage to this play is that, because the man who ran over the ball is moving toward the goal, he stands a good chance of getting to any rebounds first.

Attackers moving toward the goal, and those who line up close to the goal line, must be alert for exploitation by a watchful defense that applies an offside trap just before the ball is played forward.

FREE KICKS FROM ACUTE ANGLES

The greater the angle of the free kick, the more likely the defense will allocate most of its players in the goalmouth and fewer in a wall. There is an inclination among offensive players to line up in the prime scoring area directly in front of the opposition net. To do this is to permit the defender to mark his opponent tightly at the spot at which the attacker most desires to be free.

The attackers are better advised to position themselves *past* the far post. As the kicker runs toward the ball, the players off the ball begin their moves.

Their runs must be coordinated so that two attackers do not end up in the same place, since this brings an equal number of defenders. Remember, the more crowded the goalmouth, the easier it is to defend.

By running *onto* an incoming pass, players will get more power on their finish (be it a header or a kick), will be able to see the situation develop, enabling them to make an educated choice whether to pass to an open teammate or attempt a shot, and will have openings toward which to advance.

In addition, their movement toward the area in front of the net will draw defenders (who, it is hoped, will be a step behind them). This should create an open zone at the top of the box. The incoming ball can be headed toward the penalty circle for a predesignated attacker to shoot. Once the ball is passed backward, the advanced offensive players are susceptible to an offside trap and should therefore move away from the goal line.

CORNER KICKS

There are two basic types of corners: the *short corner kick* and the *long corner kick*. The long corner is a cross booted across the face of the goal. The short corner is a pass from the kicker to a nearby teammate who then advances toward the penalty area.

Each approach has its advantages. The short corner forces central defenders to face the flanks, making it difficult for them to watch both the ball carrier and the men they are marking. Well-timed runs off the ball or the dribbler's ability to beat defenders as he enters the penalty area can create a prime scoring opportunity. The long corner's greatest asset is that it gets the ball into a dangerous position without risking a prior loss of possession.

The Long Corner Kick

As with a free kick from an acute angle, the players off the ball line up past the far post and near the edge of the box. This allows them to run at a 45-degree angle toward the goal, making it not only easier to shoot but also to get their bodies between their marker and the ball before doing so.

One attacker should run at an angle toward where the 6 yardline intersects with the near post. One player runs toward the penalty spot, another toward the middle of the net at the 6 yardline, another toward the far post, and yet another stays wide of the far side of the goal. A few men are positioned at the top of the penalty area.

This offensive outspreading forces the defense to spread out, too, thus creating more space for shooting and maneuvering. Far too often a long corner

Correct offensive movement on a corner kick.

X1 is the kicker.

X2 supports in the event of a short corner kick. (Note: defenders must remain 10 yards from the ball until it is kicked, so X2 cannot be tightly marked.)

X3 makes a far-post run.

X4 makes a near-post run.

X5 runs to the middle of the goal.

X6 runs to the penalty spot.

X7 and X8 remain positioned to volley any weak clearances or receive a back pass.

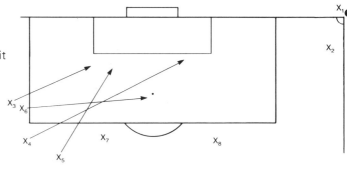

kick finds half a dozen players challenging for a cross, which makes it virtually impossible for anyone to shoot with any degree of accuracy or power. What the offense seeks to create is a one-on-one situation, making it far easier to launch a threatening shot or to pass.

Surprisingly, there are two attackers who can inflict great damage to the defense who are *not* in a position to shoot. The man running to the near post and the player positioned past the far post can be devastating offensive weapons, assuming they have the ability to head an accurate pass. As the ball is flighted into the goalmouth, defenders are drawn to it like moths to light. Attackers off the ball need merely take one step *away* from the ball to get open. If the ball is played to the near post, the player making the near-post run performs a back header. He should try to lift the ball slightly and put it across the face of the goalmouth. The reason the player making the near-post run stays 6 yards from the goal line is to prevent the keeper from intercepting his back header. A keeper is much less likely to snare a headed ball directed across the 6 yardline than he is a ball headed backward near the goal line.

If the ball is played to or beyond the far post, the offensive man heads the ball back to the opposite-sided post, also making sure his service remains at least 6 yards from the goal line. Another option is to head the ball toward the penalty arc where a couple of attackers are primed to volley a shot. These attackers are also well positioned to intercept any weak defensive clearances.

To get the ball from the corner to the goal area, there are two types of long kicks that can be used: the inswinger and the outswinger.

The Inswinger

An inswinger is a service that curves *toward* the goal line. When struck with great power and swerve, it can be used to shoot directly into the net. If the ball was at the left corner, an inswinger would result when a right-footed shooter kicked with the inside of his foot (see Banana Shot, p. 42).

The Outswinger

By contrast, the outswinger curves *away* from the goalie, and a lot of times it can fool him. The ball can appear to be coming close enough to induce the goalie to leave his line for an interception, only to swerve out of his reach. An outswinger results when the ball is kicked from the right corner with the inside of the right foot.

General Long-Corner-Kick Principles

Regardless of whether the ball is played to the near or the far post, or whether an inswinger or outswinger is used, a few rules of thumb always apply.

First, it is vital that attackers don't line up in front of the goalmouth prior to the kick.* Second, a kick that has a reasonable amount of pace gives the defense, especially the goalkeeper, less time to react. A high, lazy, floating cross is harder to head with power and much easier for a goalie to intercept. Finally, attacking players off the ball must move intelligently as a team.

To achieve all of this takes practice, lots of it. The great advantages the offense has are in knowing what it wants to do and also knowing, because the ball starts by the sideline, that defenders will have difficulty watching both the ball and their men.

The Short Corner

The same kinds of off-the-ball movement that characterize a long corner kick's success can be used on the short corner. Timing is essential: Players must not begin their movement until the ball carrier is in a good position to pass.

Unlike the long corner kick, the short corner often finds unalert attackers drawn into an offside position. On the long corner, the original kick comes from the goal line, therefore all players are onside as it is taken. When the ball is played backward to begin the short corner, the defense can employ an offside trap.

The angle of the approaching ball is different from that of a long corner kick. Since attackers wish to make an angled run onto a cross, they have to be farther from the goal line as the ball carrier approaches than they would on a long corner. The short corner is a particularly attractive option to use against a defense that has "packed" the penalty area. To boot a long cross aimlessly into such a densely populated zone is, at best, to hope for a miracle.

Logically, if the penalty area is packed, there must be inadequate numbers of defenders protecting the flanks. If the offense attacks from the side, defenders will have to abandon the goalmouth to cover the ball carrier *and* players who

*Some teams like to place one man near the keeper to challenge for the ball should it be kicked close to the goal line. All other players, however, should not be in the goalmouth before the ball is booted.

are supporting him. This creates a number of offensive possibilities: 1) the man receiving the short kick can play a wall pass with another attacker who has moved toward the ball, 2) he can draw defenders to the ball and then either pass backward to an open man at the top of the box or chip a cross pass toward the goalmouth, or 3) he can move in to take a shot himself.

There is one danger to the short corner. Should the play break down and the receiver lose the ball as he approaches the penalty area, virtually the entire team that has lost possession will be stranded upfield. This will give the opposition a great opportunity to counterattack. It is therefore critical that the ball carrier have adequate support so that he can pass the ball if challenged.

A player who supports the ball carrier (by stationing himself 5 to 10 yards farther away than the ball carrier is from the goal line, and toward the middle of the field) will have a good angle from which to dribble, shoot, or chip a far-post cross.

PENALTY KICKS

The simplest form of free kick, the penalty, should never be missed. Each team should have at least one penalty-kick specialist. He must be able to strike the ball accurately and with pace toward either post *every time.*

The number one cause of missed penalties is the kicker changing his mind at the last moment about where he wants to shoot. *Regardless of what the goalie does,* the shooter must stick with his original plan of attack.

A few tips if you find yourself taking a penalty kick:

1) Place the ball firmly on the turf so it will not move prior to the kick.
2) Know where you want to shoot and do not deviate from that plan.
3) Do not "give away" where you will shoot. As your kicking leg comes back, neither your body nor your shooting foot should move in such a way as to allow the keeper to read the direction of the shot. Not until the foot strikes the ball should the goalie find out in which direction the shot is headed.
4) Concentrate *only* on the ball and the target. What the keeper does is irrelevant. You must feel confident that if you perform your task correctly, the keeper will be powerless to make the save.

Free kicks present excellent scoring opportunities. An increasing percentage of goals in modern soccer come from set pieces, yet many coaches, inexplicably, allocate far too little training time toward them.

Of all the situations in soccer, few present as great a need in the attacking team for a balance of skill and intelligence. Free kicks need not be complicated to be successful—if the attackers know what to do and are properly trained.

7

Honing Ball Skills

Charles Hughes of the English Football Association is fond of saying, "Practice doesn't necessarily make perfect, practice makes permanent."* His point is well taken. Inadequate training technique shows glaringly in a player's shortcomings during a match.

To teach a skill in practice properly, coaches should include all of the components that will be needed to implement that skill in a game. For example, a common exercise used to improve dribbling involves players advancing the ball, slalom-style, through a series of cones. As an introduction to dribbling, this drill is fine. However, it does not require players to use deceptive body movement before touching the ball or to have an adequate range of vision so as to be aware of what is happening around the ball. Both of these skills will be needed if a player hopes to be an effective ball carrier in a game setting.

Of course, with entry-level players, drills should be simple and teach the basic touches. The cone drill is therefore a good primer to dribbling. As players become more proficient, though, the coach should introduce extra variables that add

*Speech to AYSO, Region 3 Annual General Meeting, White Plains, N.Y., Dec. 14, 1981.

Juggling is a good way to improve ball control when practicing on your own.

The cone drill. Observe how these young players look upward as they dribble and are able to use the inside and outside of both feet.

more of the components that will be needed in a match.

For example, to be a good dribbler, a player must be able to move rapidly while maintaining control of the ball with his feet. A coach can teach speed with the cone drill by having two (or more) teams engage in a relay race.

It is important that players have a good range of vision as they dribble. One way to force them to look up, during a relay race, is to position the coach in front of the cones. When he raises his hand, the players with the ball can proceed directly back to their waiting teammates, skipping the remaining cones. Teammates are not allowed to call out instructions. The ball carrier who is slow to see the coach's uplifted arm will lose precious time.

There are now only two main match components left: body swerve and deciding whether to pass, dribble, or shoot.

Body swerve can be taught by having players go one-on-one in a confined area. Small-sided scrimmages and drills (also discussed in the next chapter) can also be used to teach judgment under gamelike conditions. In general, drills that teach skills must incorporate as many game elements as possible to be of any real value to the player.

DRIBBLING DRILLS

The cone drill is but one of several exercises used to improve dribbling technique. A good introduction to dribbling involves placing a ball between a player's feet. Standing on his toes, the player alternates lifting feet while tapping the ball from one foot to the other.

As youngsters begin to feel comfortable with a ball, they can try jogging with a ball at their feet. The next step is to engage in "follow the leader." A coach or an advanced teammate stands in front of a line of players, each separated by 5 to 10 yards, with everyone having his own ball. The line then

This useful passing drill has the player in the middle run to receive a pass from his teammate in the foreground, play a wall pass back to the server, and then move toward his other partner to repeat the procedure.

trots around the field with all participants required to duplicate the maneuvers of their leader.

PASSING DRILLS

There is a variety of simple exercises that can help players learn to pass accurately and with the proper pace on the first touch. These can follow a logical progression that allows a neophyte to improve at a comfortable rate while experiencing a minimum of failure.*

The most simple passing drill has two players face each other and kick the ball back and forth.

The next step is to have two lines of players facing each other, about 10 yards apart. The first player, in line one, passes the ball to his counterpart in line two. After he makes the pass, the player from line one runs to the back of the other line. Meanwhile, the receiver traps the ball on the first touch and passes it to the player who is now at the front of the first line.

Once players feel comfortable foot-trapping the ball, they are ready to try executing first-touch passes.

Another option is to play "monkey in the middle." Two players stand 15 to 25 yards apart, each with a ball, while a teammate stands between them. The man in the middle runs toward one of his teammates, who passes him the ball. The receiver plays it back on the first touch, pivots, and runs toward his other teammate to repeat the procedure.

Once these drills have been mastered, a coach can introduce a slightly more advanced wall-pass exercise, also using two facing lines. The first player in line one runs to a spot between the two lines. The first player in line two passes the ball and runs forward and to the side of the receiver to accept a

*It is important, especially at the youth level, that players engage in drills in which they improve yet are not subjected to an excessive amount of confidence-shattering failures.

The circle drill sharpens offensive passing and promotes sound defensive technique.

first-touch return pass. As he re-collects the ball, the player from line two strikes a first-touch pass to the man at the head of line one. Both players advance to the back of the other line. As the man from line two gives the ball to the first player in line one, another man from line two runs to the middle and the exercise is repeated. On all of these drills, players should use the inside and outside of both feet.

When intermediate-level players can perform these passing drills, they are ready for small-sided drills. Perhaps the most popular is a game of keepaway in which the attackers form a circle of four to six players that surround two defenders. The attackers must keep the ball moving rapidly, preferably by passing on the initial touch. The defenders in the middle try to win the ball. When a defender makes an interception, the passer and the receiver who lost the ball exchange places with the men in the middle.

Another favorite is to have six attackers line up around the center circle with four defensive players on the inside. This exercise can be turned into a fun game in which the offensive players are awarded a point for a set number of consecutive passes and two points for every penetrating pass (a pass that is struck to a teammate at the opposite side of the circle). The defense is given a point for an interception or any time an errant pass leaves the area.

Skill at longer passes, such as the instep pass, can be sharpened by making two players strike balls to each other over a fair distance. As proficiency improves, a defender can be added to mark the receiver. The player off the ball must thus get free, while the ball carrier is forced to make an accurate pass.

In another drill, the ball is placed just inside the penalty area. Three offensive players, faced with two defenders, try to get clear for a pass. The ball carrier, who can't leave the penalty box (but is free to move around within it), is given a specific amount of time to complete a pass to a teammate. The receiver must bring the ball under control for it to count as a completion. The only stipulation is that the pass must leave the ground.

Players alternate and points are awarded for successful passes (for the offense) and for unsuccessful passes or interceptions (for the defense). The offensive player must not only control the ball but must do so within the area bounded by the midfield line, the sidelines, and the edge of the penalty area.

A variation on the same theme involves two rectangles 20 by 30 yards that are 25 yards apart. In each grid are three attacking players and either one or two defenders. Dribbling is prohibited and at least one out of every five passes must travel from one rectangle to the other.

SHOOTING DRILLS

The greatest criticism of the North American player is his alleged inability to "make things happen" in the attacking third of the field. Of particular concern are our shortcomings in the penalty area, especially when it comes to finishing chances. But if you ever saw a typical North American practice in which shooting drills are included, it's easy to see why this deficiency exists.

An appalling number of teams on all levels are content to limit shooting practice to striking stationary balls from the edge of the penalty area with only a goalie protecting the net. To teach finishing in such a manner is as futile as a basketball coach teaching outside shooting with nothing but uncontested lay-up drills.

Sure, it's fine for the beginner to hit a dead ball on goal, but that situation just does not happen in a game. Players must learn to strike balls that are moving, that are coming from all angles, that are taking bad hops or arriving in midair. Players should practice while subjected to defensive pressure, and with little time or space to take their shots.

The first step in teaching players how to shoot is to put them in a line facing the goal, with the front person about 30 yards from the net. A server stands at the top of the penalty circle. The player in the front of the line passes to the server, who then strikes a first-touch square pass. The shooter must run onto the ball and *shoot on the initial touch*. The server should strike the ball to either

A   B

In this helpful shooting drill, the attacker passes to a server (A), who rolls a wall pass for the attacker to run onto (B). The shooter must strike the ball on the first touch (C, D). As players improve, the server makes shooting more challenging by lifting the ball in the

side, thereby forcing shooters to use both feet. As finishing improves, the server can flick passes so that the shooter must strike the ball while it is bouncing. Later, a defender can be introduced. His job is to run at the shooter but offer only minimal resistance. His appearance brings urgency to the finish, forcing the shooter to shoot around the defender to avoid having his shot blocked.

Not all scoring opportunities occur with the shooter able to run onto the ball as he faces the net. It is a far tougher proposition to hit the ball in a different direction than the one he is facing. To teach this valued skill, the line of shooters starts at the corner of the penalty area. The ball is served from the opposite side. At first, simple ground balls are passed for the shooter to kick. As proficiency increases, bouncing balls and then aerial crosses are struck. This type of finish requires the player to strike the ball on the first touch, to time his movements and get over the ball in such a manner that the shot is powerful and stays low, and to be aware of his position vis-à-vis the goal and the keeper at the moment he shoots.

Even with this relatively advanced drill, the skills tested are not as challenging as those demanded in match conditions. In a shooting drill, the player is aware that a scoring chance is upcoming and can anticipate the type of shot (instep drive, volley, half-volley, etc.) that will be most appropriate. In a game, things happen much faster. Thus, the best method to improve shooting is the small-sided game, or drills in which the scoring opportunity must be earned and taken in a manner similar to a match (see Chapter 8).

C

D

air or passing wide. The server should pass to either side of the field so players can learn to use both feet.

PENALTY KICK PRACTICE

The best way to prepare to take a penalty kick in a match is through repetition in practice. To improve accuracy, the shooter can place sticks or cones on the goal line a yard to the inside of each goalpost. The shooter must then kick the ball between the stick and the post.

TRAPPING DRILLS

To play soccer with any degree of proficiency, players must be able to bring the ball under control on the first touch. The art of trapping, be it with the foot, thigh, chest, or head, is one of the first skills a beginner should seek to master.

The easiest way to start is by pairing players off. At first, players kick grounders to each other, stopping the ball with the inside of the foot. From there a progression occurs, with one player serving balls at thigh, and later, chest and head height.

More mature players can introduce other components to this drill. To perform a trap in a game, a player needs to position his body so that it is perpendicular to the ball's line of flight. He must shield his opponent and control the ball quickly on the first touch in a manner that will allow him to be ready to play it on the second touch. Further, the ball must land in a spot where it can *only* be played by the receiver or a teammate.

The best soccer drills duplicate match conditions. In this drill, the receiver must not only perform a chest trap, he must first move into the ball's line of flight while shielding his marker from the ball. The addition of opponents teaches him to direct the ball *away* from defenders while maintaining close control so he can pass or dribble immediately.

To teach these ingredients, coaches can serve a ball to a player "on offense" from varying angles and distances. A defender marking the receiver offers modest resistance to force the offensive player to maintain good tight control. As the receiver improves his skill, he can practice passing the ball back to the server on the second touch or turning and trying to dribble past the defender.

HEADING PRACTICE

It is only natural for the young player to be reluctant to bang his head into a ball. Before a player can learn correct heading technique, he must overcome his fears. How to do it?

The first step is for a player to hold the ball with both hands at forehead height and gently toss it against the hairline so he learns to use that part of the head. Players soon realize that it doesn't hurt to head a ball correctly. Step two involves jumping up to head a ball suspended by a string from a pole or tree branch.

The third step is for two players to toss balls lightly to each other from 5 to 10 yards away. At this point coaches should be especially alert in observing

To get a feel for heading, start by tossing the ball gently against your forehead in easy repetitions.

if proper technique is maintained. The transition from step two to step three often finds players closing their eyes prematurely. As a result, the ball hits too high on the head or strikes the nose. Those youngsters who can't successfully negotiate this modest transition may have to regress slightly. They should first learn to head balls that are served lightly from only a couple of yards away before proceeding further. In time, players will snap their upper bodies so that the ball flies back on a line to the server. To lessen a youngster's anxieties, you may wish to slightly deflate the balls to make them softer.

Head Tennis

Once players are absolutely comfortable with heading the ball, they're ready to try a terrific practice aid, head tennis. For fun and skill enhancement, no other training device in soccer equals this exhilarating exercise. Its rules are similar to volleyball, with the exceptions that players may not use their hands or arms, the ball may touch the ground once before it is sent over the net, and the height of the net can vary (it is usually from 1 to 3 feet). Despite its name, head tennis calls on its participants to use all parts of the anatomy, save for hands and arms. Although it can be played on a tennis court (using the service and singles sidelines as boundaries), head tennis is most often played anywhere that four players can find a bench to function as a net.

1980 NASL Coach of the Year Alan Hinton credits the liberal use of head tennis for much of his club's success. In their final week of preparation for Soccer Bowl '82, Hinton's Seattle Sounders began every training session by engaging in spirited head-tennis matches.

Head tennis makes practice fun.

PRACTICING THROW-INS

This skill should be relatively easy to learn, owing to its similarity to techniques used in other popular North American sports.

Once again players are paired off. The distance of their throws should vary so that players feel as comfortable tossing a ball 30 yards as they do 5 yards. On short throws, players must be sure that they bring the ball all the way behind the head and complete the follow-through. On longer services they must be careful to keep both feet on the ground and on or behind the sideline until after the throwing motion has been completed.*

CONDITIONING

Not until players reach their teenage years should a coach begin to concern himself with physical conditioning. The only calisthenics that younger players need to perform are some stretching exercises at the start of training or prior to a game. Even though the danger of pulled or strained muscles is minimal with children, they should get in the habit of warming up before engaging in any strenuous activity.

Not surprisingly, the most helpful conditioning tool in soccer is running. Owing to the demands of a match, players need to develop stamina and the ability to accelerate over short distances. Estimates vary, but most agree that an outfield player can look forward to a minimum of 5 miles of running over the duration of a 90-minute match. As such, long-distance training is helpful, particularly during preseason workouts.

Many coaches mistakenly feel that cross-country work is sufficient to prepare their squads. Although running several miles does improve stamina, it does not simulate the type of movement that soccer demands. Many times in matches, players are called upon to burst into a sprint, return to a jog, change direction, backpedal, jump, and then sprint again. This constant stopping, turning, and starting requires a far greater expenditure of energy than does jogging at a steady pace. When soccer coaches say that a player has good "speed," they are alluding to his ability to accelerate over a short distance.

That's why teams even on the professional level include a variety of running drills in their daily activities. A good exercise is to have players jog around the field. On hearing the coach's whistle they must sprint until hearing a second whistle, at which point they again jog. On the second lap they must jump to head an imaginary ball when the whistle sounds. Subsequent laps can find them backpedaling on signal.

*See rules for throw-ins on pages 21 and 56.

In another drill, players lie on the ground, and, when the whistle blows, they jump up and sprint over a short, predetermined distance.

"Shuttles" (also known as "lines") is an exercise in which players run to touch the 5 yardline, run back to touch the starting line, and then run to the 10 yardline and back, etc. (until they run to the 25 yardline and return). The high-school-varsity age player should be able to run ten shuttles in 35 to 40 seconds or less, with a 35-to-40-second rest between shuttles.

In addition to working on cardiovascular conditioning, players should perform exercises to strengthen their leg muscles. In one popular drill, players run while carrying a teammate piggy back–style, and in another, players move in various directions, touching the ground with one hand, then the other, while in a deep crouch.

A   B

Warm-up stretching is a must in soccer. Exercises can be made more interesting by introducing a teammate and a ball (A, B). In (C), the hands roll the ball around the legs in a figure-8 pattern.

C

In a game, the length of a player's strides will vary. When he is running at full speed he will take longer strides than when he is trying to dribble around an opponent. The Brazilians have an exercise in which field lines (or sticks laid down) are used to force players to take very short strides or long ones.

Strong abdominal muscles are also needed in soccer. Obviously, doing plenty of regular sit-ups can help. In a less tedious form of sit-ups, two teammates face each other while lying on the ground with the soles of their shoes touching. The first player sits up and hands the ball to her partner. The teammate then performs a sit-up, taking the ball over her head with both hands until it touches the ground before returning it.

Another abdominal conditioner begins with the player seated. He must twist his body so that his left forearm touches the turf to the right side of the body and vice versa.

Leg lifts are equally helpful. One player lies on his back with his arms fully extended past his head. His hands grip the ankles of a partner who is standing behind him. The man on the ground must kick his legs upward to touch his partner's arms (which are held in front of the chest). The standing player then pushes his teammate's feet downward. The man on the ground must stop his heels before they touch the turf and then repeat the procedure.

More two-player exercises? Standing back-to-back, two players hand the ball back and forth. Player A reaches to his right to give the ball to player B. Player B then twists from the waist to give the ball back as player A reaches to his left to receive the return. Players keep both hands on the ball to force a full turn of the body. From there, the players can alternate handing the ball through their legs and over their heads.

PRACTICING ALONE

As noted in the Preface, all that is needed to play soccer is "a boy, a ball, and a wall." (Actually, that old axiom should be amended to read "a boy or a *girl*, a ball, and a wall.")

If you find yourself alone and itching to practice, juggling a soccer ball is a great way to sharpen your skill without the aid of teammates. The idea is to prevent the ball from touching the ground by using any and all parts of your body, except, of course, the hands or arms. Not only does juggling help you learn to control the ball, it also improves your balance and your belief that you are the master of the ball. University of Connecticut coach Joe Morrone requires each of his players pass a juggling test in which they must be able to complete 50 successful touches with each foot, 100 with both; 50 with each thigh and 100 with both; 100 with the head; and 200 overall. Although there are very few instances in a game in which a player will actually touch the ball consecutively more than once in the air, Coach Morrone knows that if a player can juggle at least 50 times with his weaker foot, he can be counted upon to complete a 10-yard pass successfully with that foot.

You can further improve your basic skills by using a wall or a soccer bangboard. Run parallel to it, passing the ball (with pace) off the wall with the inside and outside of both feet, and keep running to collect the return pass. Just before passing or receiving the return, you can add a feint to your movements to "fool" an imaginary opponent.

While facing the wall, try kicking the ball in the air, and learn to control the return with your chest, thigh, or foot. You can also use the wall for heading practice. Start by heading the ball high on the wall and then strike the return downward. See how many consecutive off-the-wall touches you can complete (using your head, chest, thighs, and feet) without the ball striking the turf.

A wall is an excellent aid for improving your finishing skills. Standing some distance from the wall, kick the ball against it so that the return bounces to either side of you. Try then to strike a first-touch shot. By using either foot and by hitting the ball against a specific target area on the wall, you learn to shoot both powerfully and accurately on the initial touch.

If a friend is available, the two of you can practice other "off-the-wall" soccer skills. Let one of you be the offensive player who kicks the ball against

There's no limit to the skills two teammates can practice together.

the wall and then must collect the return. To do this, you must legally shield the other person from the ball. After gaining possession, try to turn and dribble around the defender. The more advanced player you are, the more you can challenge yourself by kicking the ball to the side and/or high off of the wall.

With a second person you can also practice without a wall. Try, for instance, juggling in tandem, passing the ball back and forth without allowing it to touch the ground. Play keepaway to improve your shielding skill with the ball. (Keepaway can also be played with the attacker allowed to use the wall as his "teammate," which helps him learn to pass, move for the return, shield his marker off the ball, and gain possession while under pressure.)

SKILL AIDS

In addition to using a wall, there are a lot of commercial skill aids that can help improve individual skills. They range from beanbag-like sacks (used for juggling) to bounce-back nets (for improving first-touch skills and control). If you're on a budget, you can improvise with less expensive aids. The great Pelé is able to juggle an orange with ease. If you can learn to control a tennis ball, for instance, think how much easier juggling and passing skills will be when using a full-sized soccer ball.

One of the great joys of soccer is that you can enjoy playing it by yourself in the backyard or park just as much as in a full-sided game. Unlike many sports, you can improve noticeably without the company of others. Furthermore, by setting and reaching personal goals, you can chart your improvement.

Not until you have a good grasp of the fundamental skills are you prepared to participate in scrimmages or games. Once the basic skills have been acquired, you are ready to attempt the intricate collective skills and movements that are demanded in a match.

Team Practice

A vital factor separating exceptional from average players is the ability to recognize instantly all components in the decision-making process and respond appropriately to best exploit the situation.

As soccer's participatory level has continued to mushroom, more players can now adequately execute the basic skills needed to play the game at their age level. Often missing, however, are the mental attributes required to be a good player.

If you're a coach, you must recognize this and devise ways of preparing your players physically *and* mentally, both individually and as a team. This is best accomplished through following a logical progression when teaching the game.

1) Teach the young player the physical steps necessary to implement a skill.
2) Have the young player practice that skill in isolation until such time as he or she can adequately perform it.
3) Organize drills that involve the use of closely related skills, so that those skills become second nature in a game situation.
4) Organize small-sided drills, scrimmages, and condition games to stress both ball skills and decision-making proficiency in gamelike situations.

Team meetings are excellent times for coaches to demonstrate new skills or correct common mistakes.

We have already discussed the various practice exercises designed to polish basic ball skills. The next step is the hardest: a player must take what he has learned in training into match conditions. Far too frequently players choose to implement an inappropriate skill while under game stress. They dribble when a pass would be more effective, or they play the ball forward when a back pass is in order.

The soccer world is full of excellent practice players who are incapable of reproducing that form in a match. Often, the failure to negotiate that transition is the result of having neglected to learn the game's skills in small steps. A player must first master the basic skills, then use them in drills, small-sided games, scrimmages, and finally, a real game.

There are many tools that you as coach can use in helping your charges learn to utilize their skills in a game. All of them bring simulated match conditions into a confined space.

THE GRID SYSTEM

Invariably during the course of a contest there are isolated confrontations of limited numbers of players. One-on-one, two-on-one, two-on-two, three-on-two, and three-on-three duels constantly arise. The team that best handles these situations stands an excellent chance of winning.

Players must learn how they can gain numerical advantages as well as how to exploit those advantages. One of the best ways of teaching numerical exploitation is using a practice procedure known as the *grid system*.

The training ground is divided into a series of rectangles. Within each area different numerical confrontations take place. The size of the grids vary: larger grids for lesser-skilled players, smaller ones for the more advanced athletes. A common size is 10 by 10 yards.

One-on-One

There are two types of one-on-one exercises.

In the first, players play keepaway. One player has the ball while the other tries to take it from him. The man in possession learns how to shield his marker while still maintaining good close control. In an attempt to win the ball, the defender will try to jockey his opponent toward the sideline and/or onto his weaker foot. Further, the defender learns how and when to tackle.

It is important that you as coach watch to be sure neither man develops bad habits. The dribbler, for instance, may tend to look at the ball. The marker may start to tackle wrecklessly, knowing, if he misses in this drill, he can always catch up to his opponent because of the limited space of the grid. Offenders can be "punished" with a lap around the field or a few pushups for any such indiscretion.

A variation on the keepaway theme involves the use of a small goal. It should be only a foot or two wide, thus forcing a player to dribble around his rival in order to have a reasonable chance of scoring. This exercise encourages attacking players to take opponents on.

Two-on-One

An important lesson in soccer is that a player's responsibilities do not end after he releases the ball. As soon as a pass is made, he must move intelligently either to receive a return pass or to create space for a teammate.

Two-on-one grid play teaches the offensive participants to analyze where space will develop and move to it instantly to receive a return pass. It teaches the defender to "force" bad passes by making attackers use their weaker foot or rush their passes. And, because of its limited playing area, it demands accurate, properly paced passes.

By prohibiting players from dribbling, it greatly aids first-touch passing skills. As with the three-on-two grid situation, the offensive objective is to maintain possession.

Two-on-Two

Like the one-on-one, two-on-two confrontations have two variations: keepaway and using goals. The former is excellent for teaching offensive and defensive supporting, while the latter emphasizes wall passes and a quick transition game.

Three-on-Two

Offensively, three-on-two practice stresses good close control and off-the-ball movement. Defensively, teamwork comes into play. One defensive player makes an angled approach to the ball carrier, thus forcing the direction of his pass, while the second defender reads the situation and positions himself for an interception. To avoid losing possession, the attackers must play the ball quickly and accurately. The limited grid size forces them to improve their skills. In addition, they learn how to move to break down the play into a two-on-one confrontation as well as to think a couple of passes ahead.

Overview

The beauty of the grid system is that it teaches and hones physical and mental skill, improves fitness, and yet is fun. And coaches, you can add extra competitive incentives. In one-on-one or two-on-two keepaway games, let the winner(s) be determined by total time of possession. In two-on-one or three-on-two keepaway contests, award a point to the defense for an interception and one to the offense for completing a specific number of consecutive passes.

Because modern soccer demands all-around skills from all its participants, all players should get an opportunity to perform offensively and defensively in all variations involved. Every 5 minutes, make players switch from one grid to another.

SMALL-SIDED DRILLS

To take advantage of scoring opportunities, players must know how to play intelligently and quickly in the attacking third of the field, where time and space are at a premium. A good way to teach such soccer "smarts" is to use half-field drills. These incorporate a keeper and a regulation-size goal to force attackers to shoot in circumstances similar to those found in a match.

Five on Four

Five-on-four, or six-on-four half-field play benefits the offensive and defensive players equally.

The defense tries to force its adversaries to go wide while covering attackers near the ball and in front of the net so that the attackers can only make long passes (which are harder to complete).

The offense counters such pressure with a quick, short-passing game. To accomplish this, players must move intelligently off the ball and correctly make split-second decisions while in possession.

The attackers try to lure the defenders away from the most dangerous shooting zones. Once that has been accomplished, they quickly change their point of attack to best isolate an outnumbered defender in the center of the field.

In the diagram, the offense has gotten the ball forward to its winger (X1), who is near the touchline. The right midfielder (X2) has taken up an intelligent supporting position, 10 yards behind his teammate and at an angle that not only makes him easily available for a pass, but also yields the maximum number of favorable options after he receives the ball.

Meanwhile, the striker (X3) has moved toward the ball and, by doing this, he has taken his defender with him, thus creating attacking space for X4 and X5 to exploit later.

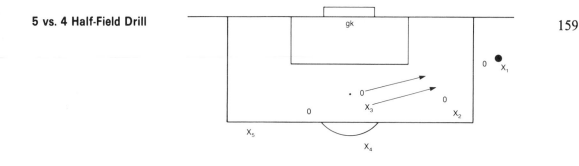

Seeing the play develop, X1 can either play the ball to X2—who is in a better position to pass to X4 or X5—or X1 can pass to X3. Should the pass go to X3, the striker, then X2 can make an angled run into the box to receive a first-touch pass from him.

If X1 decides to pass to his supporting midfielder (X2), a number of other options arise. X2 can play a wall pass with X3, running to the inside to receive a return that could result in either a shot or an easy pass to X4 or X5 if the central defender comes to mark him. X2 could also continue the sequence by dribbling directly into the penalty area, especially if X3's run has pulled his defender so far out of position that he will be unable to pick up X2 as he moves on goal.

No matter which avenue is pursued, the result should be the same: a ball carrier is set free to run at the near post. As the player in possession approaches the goal, X4 delays his run forward. This will leave the ball carrier a good passing angle should the central defender move quickly enough to deny him a shot. Had X4 rushed forward, as is the inclination of most young players, the only way to get him the ball would be to loft a pass over the ball carrier's marker, which is not only more difficult to execute but also allows the keeper a chance to intercept the cross.

What happens if X3's marker is intelligent enough not to vacate prime attacking space by following his man?

In that situation, X3 is open. The ball is immediately played to him so that he can run at his defender. X2 moves to support at the top of the penalty area (and should be open for a shot). However, if X3 passes backward, he must be wary not to be drawn offside by an alert defense.

As you can see, regardless of what X3's marker does, the offense should be able to create a good scoring opportunity. The five-on-four teaches attacking patience as well. There are times when the offense will have to change the direction of the attack in order to isolate a defender.

Three on Two

This equation is a good alternative for less advanced players who may not yet be capable of properly executing the skill and quick thinking demanded by five-on-four or six-on-four drills, yet it allows players to practice movements useful in real games.

Here is a typical three-on-two play. It begins with the central attacker (X1) in possession (see A). He passes to either wing and then runs around the *back* of the receiver (X2). Doing so isolates the defender on that side (O1). In addition, by running *behind* the winger, the player is never in an offside position and has a better angle from which to receive a penetrating pass.

As X1 moves around his teammate, X2 "attacks" the defender, running right at him. O1 is now forced to make a no-win decision. He must either mark the ball carrier (thus leaving X1 open for a dangerous downfield pass) or retreat to cover the passing alley (thus allowing X2 to run past him, creating a two-on-one confrontation at the top of the penalty box).

If the latter occurs, X3 delays his forward movement. He is careful neither to advance into an offside position nor to allow the defender to negate his presence by blocking the passer's path to the receiver.

If the ball is played down the line for X1, X3 times a near-post run so that he crosses the goalmouth just as X1 receives the ball. Meanwhile, X2 runs behind X3 and into prime shooting space (see B).

Now the central defender has a dilemma: he must go with X3, leaving X2 dangerously unguarded. Note that X2 does not rush to the 6-yard box. Instead, he lines up so that X3 can dummy the ball through to him (see C). By leaving space to run into, the cross does not come close enough for the keeper to intercept.

Strange as it may seem, the three-on-two is also an excellent device for teaching defensive tactics.

The defender at the initial point of attack (O1) uses body feints to try to trick the ball carrier. As the play begins, O1 is a good distance from both X1 and X2. Decreasing that space considerably as the first pass is struck, O1 pretends to attack the ball before X1 has completed his run behind X2 (that is, before X1 is headed downfield. He has not yet begun to move toward the space into which a pass may be played).

By lowering his shoulder and taking a half-step forward (toward X2), O1 makes X2 think (incorrectly!) that a penetrating pass is appropriate. If O1 can force that pass to be struck prematurely, he may be able to beat X1 to the ball.

Another defensive option is for O1 to force X2 to pass to the overlapping X1. Reading the play, O2 slides toward the corner to mark X1. O1 retreats toward the near post, assuming a position between the remaining two attackers.

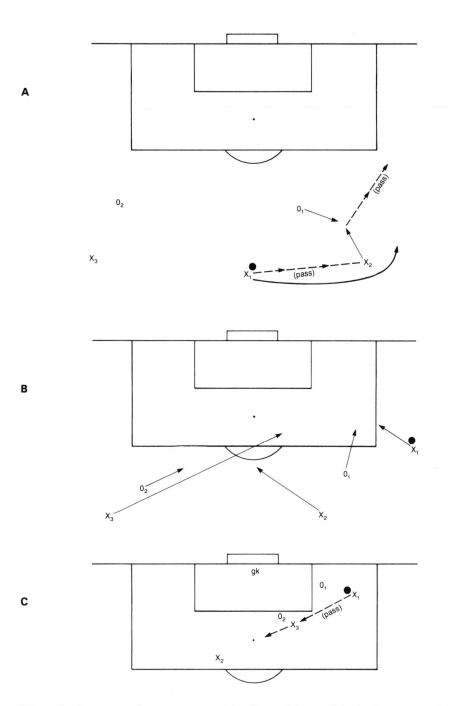

Thus, he hopes to force a cross that 1) could possibly be intercepted by the keeper, 2) could be inaccurate, owing to the difficulty of hitting a long pass while running at full speed, or 3) will be tougher for the receiver to control and shoot quickly.

Under no circumstance should either of the two defenders be able to steal the ball *if* the attackers do their job. *But,* by playing intelligently, the defense can make their opponents not only attempt difficult passes but also a greater number of them. This increases the chance of an offensive error and also buys time in a match situation until defensive reinforcements can arrive.

Overview

Coaches often neglect half-field drills, a primary reason for the inability of many skillful teams to translate midfield dominance into goals.

There are many numerical variations that can be used. Regardless of whether you opt to use seven attackers or only three, it is important that you maintain a relative equality between defensive and offensive players.

Many teams at the youth and scholastic levels will work on five-on-two confrontations. Not only is this extremely unrealistic (how often during the course of a season, let alone one match, would such a lopsided match-up occur?), it also fosters bad habits. When things are too easy for the attackers, they can get sloppy in their passing and/or finishing and still put the ball in the net. They refuse to attempt the half-chance, waiting instead for the "perfect" scoring opportunity to develop. And since they feel as if they have all day to shoot, they learn to take as much time as they want before striking the ball. When players get in a game, these habits will conspire against them. It is *vital* that all scoring opportunities in practice be *earned,* for they will not come easily in a match.

SMALL-SIDED GAMES

An equally useful training tool is the small-sided game. Playing on a half-field (or less) with no more than six players per team affords each player twice the touches he would get in an eleven-a-side game. With the exception of long passing, all the skills of a regulation match are required of each individual, only far more often.

The scaled-down game is a particularly good exercise for youngsters. Playing full-sided games on an adult-sized field can overwhelm the immature athlete. Often, such contests deteriorate into a glorified form of kickball in which everyone chases after the ball with the winner of the race booting it aimlessly upfield. The small-sided game, a microcosm of the real thing, has the advantage of building skills while discouraging the types of bad habits that

The 3-vs.-3 small-sided game is an extremely helpful training device that can improve a team's transition game as well as its goalkeeping, passing, and finishing skills.

eleven-a-side soccer can instill in young players. Many college and professional sides feature small-sided training to aid team play in confined areas.

Three-on-Three

This game uses six outfield players, a 40-by-30-yard surface, and regulation-size goals that are manned by keepers. As fast-paced as indoor soccer, it provides great work for the goalies while improving finishing, man-to-man marking skills, and the transition game.

On a small field, players are forced to shoot whenever a half-chance appears. Those who hesitate will find the opportunity lost. With ball possession changing rapidly, players must be alert and make the adjustment from offense to defense (and vice versa). Three-on-three games force defenders to attack and attackers to defend. They prohibit players from being lax in areas other than their speciality and from delegating any of their responsibilities to teammates.

Indiana University coach Jerry Yeagley not only credits this exercise with greatly aiding his team's finishing abilities, he feels it has equal defensive merits. By initiating "forced marking" (i.e., having each player responsible for one opponent), he has taken players with glaring defensive weaknesses and made them more than adequate in this important aspect of the game. A prime example is Chicago Sting standout Rudy Glenn. When Rudy arrived at IU, he was a striker who wasn't terribly concerned about what happened when the Hoosiers didn't have possession. After a few sessions of three-on-three in which Glenn's man scored some goals, Rudy's pride was aroused. Annoyed at being embarrassed defensively, he made himself into a good all-around player. After turning pro, Glenn was moved to the midfield, where his ability to mark dangerous rivals, as well as attack, played a key role in the Sting's triumphant 1981 outdoor season.

Five-on-Five

Using a 50-by-40-yard field, five-on-five (plus keepers) underscores intelligent off-the-ball movement. If teammates fail to support each other, allowing the ball carrier to make a simple pass, the resulting breakdown will often be punished by a goal on the counterattack.

Five-on-five hones close control in tight quarters and forces players to think, perform skillfully, and convert half-chances.

Five-on-Five (Without Goals)

In this drill, teams earn points by making a consecutive number of passes without losing possession. Without goals, players are encouraged to spread apart, making maximum use of space through off-the-ball movement. This is extremely good practice for forwards, who learn to face the ball and to leave space for themselves to move into as they run to support the ball carrier. The more advanced the players' skill levels are, the smaller the boundaries should be.

CONDITION GAMES

The final step in the progression from isolated skill drills to match conditions are eleven-a-side practice games. These scrimmages are ideal for ironing out minor kinks.

An alternative to the intrasquad scrimmage is the condition game, governed by the same laws as a match, with one specific rule change. That alteration can be any of a number of conditions, each designated to promote a specific aspect of team play.

For example, if a side that features a strong passing game finds that its players either lack the ability or inclination to dribble, a condition may be imposed that each ball carrier must dribble past at least one opponent before he is permitted to pass or shoot. Should any player pass or shoot without first performing the mandated condition, the other team is awarded an indirect free kick and the guilty party must run a lap.

There are many popular condition games, some of which are outlined below. It is worth noting that conditions such as one- or two-touch play can also be applied to small-sided games and drills with positive results.

Limited-Touch Soccer

One of the favorite tools of coaches on the collegiate and professional levels is the use of one- and two-touch soccer. Players are limited to making contact with the ball (with *any* part of their body) no more than one or two times per possession.

The high skill level demanded of one-touch soccer may be too advanced for many college and almost all high-school teams. However, two-touch play can reap great benefits, both to teams and individuals.

Ideal for teams of high-school age or above, it encourages players to employ deceptive body movement *before* their initial touch of the ball. By learning to *appear* to move (or pass) in one direction before moving the opposite way on the initial touch, players create valuable space for themselves.

Too, limiting the number of touches forces players to think a few steps ahead, both on and off the ball. They must support each other intelligently while functioning as a unit.

Four-Goal Soccer

A universal shortcoming among young players is the tendency to see openings *only* in front of them. They must learn to sense the space to the side and in back of them, and to use it (known as getting width and depth into the attack).

To do this, try a four-goal variation of the eleven-a-side game. Adding a goal on each sideline and widening the field by 10 to 30 yards (if possible) opens a new dimension to the game. Each team has to defend two goals, one on the goal line and one on a sideline. The two extra goalies bring the total number of participants to twenty-four.

A team can score by shooting the ball into either of their opponent's two goals, and thus learn to change the point of their attack from one side of the field to the other.

Players' vision should improve noticeably playing four-goal soccer. Those players on the far side of the field are discouraged from bunching toward the ball. And defenders away from the point of the attack must be alert to all that is happening around them.

Directional Passing

To enhance patience in attacking, place a condition on the direction of passes. Mandate, for example, that every set number of passes must be struck backward or sideways before the ball can again be played forward.

This condition teaches players not to go forward all of the time. Many young attackers force the issue, moving ahead even though badly outnumbered. Furthermore, players off the ball have a tendency to sprint toward the net. At least some of them must remain to the side and behind the ball, not only so that back passes can be made if needed but also to prevent the penalty area from becoming overcrowded.

By having men behind the ball, the attacking team is better able to make the transition to defense should it lose possession.

Heading All Shots

To improve both offensive and defensive heading in the penalty area, stipulate that a goal may only be scored by heading the ball into the net. In this way wingers and overlapping defenders derive tremendous benefit from crossing the ball, and the attacking team learns to use the entire width of the field.

Variations

Obviously, there are as many conditions for such games as there are flaws to be remedied.

With their similarity to a match, such condition scrimmages allow coaches to better evaluate their players. And, best of all, players find condition games, as they do the grid system, a stimulating form of training; they apply themselves to practice enthusiastically, thus nurturing that essential ingredient for team and personal improvement: spirit.

Goalkeeping Practice

Goalkeepers should be segregated during a good part of a practice so they can learn and develop the unique skills that their position demands.

Younger keepers should concentrate on the fundamentals, such as catching the ball correctly and getting their upper body behind the shot. They can also work on catching and punching crosses as well as on punting and throwing the ball.

As their body muscles mature, keepers can practice their diving technique. Not until the average child is in his midteens can he be expected to have the power to propel his body into a dive with any degree of proficiency.

If you're a goalie, your top training priority should be executing proper technique. Goalies can get into bad habits (that will haunt them as they move into higher levels of competition in later years) by making one-handed desperation saves in practice. In drills, your coach should encourage you to strive for good technical performance. Keep in mind that during practice it is far better to miss the ball or drop it *while trying to make a two-handed catch* than merely to deflect the ball from danger. In a game, instinct takes over, and you will have no trouble making the parry save. If,

169

Good goalkeeping form is a result of specialized training.

however, you get in the habit of deflecting instead of catching shots in practice, you will never learn how to play goal properly!

WARMING UP

After engaging in basic stretching exercises, you are ready to begin your work with the aid of a ball, a server, and a second teammate.

Start by lying on your stomach, facing the server, while the second teammate firmly holds your ankles to the ground. Have the server gently toss balls to you from a distance of 3 to 5 yards. The services should be a foot or two off the ground, to either side, or directly above you. Make your catch with both hands, but without using your hands or arms to push your upper body off the ground. This is a very good warm-up drill for getting the feel of the ball and limbering up the lower back. After a few sets of ten or so catches, you are ready for a slightly more challenging exercise.

Sit with your legs together in front of you. Have the server stand 5 yards away and lightly kick shots to either side of your body. Make all your saves with *both hands*.

Next, stand up and roll the ball to the server. Let him start by taking soft shots from 5 to 10 yards out. These are easy saves to give you the feel of the ball and to get loose. You should not try to do any diving just yet. As you become ready, the server's shots should force you to leave your feet. At first, the shots should be within a few feet of your body. Although you must dive

A helpful warm-up drill involves a server, a holder, and the goalie.

to make the play, your hands are able to catch the ball within the chest region.
Slowly, let the difficulty of the shots progress so that you must extend yourself.
You are now ready for the training session.

ANGLE WORK

If you're a young keeper, you should dedicate considerable time to angle work.
One simple, yet effective, exercise involves you and your coach. Your coach
dribbles a ball around the outskirts of the penalty area. You assume the position
you would take to protect against a shot. The coach should be able to see an
equal amount of net on either side of you.

One common error among young goalies is that they overcompensate on
angles. As the shooter moves a few steps to one side, the inexperienced keeper
will often match him stride for stride. Before long, the entire goal is exposed.
When this happens, the coach should switch positions with the goalie, allowing
the keeper to see his error. This approach is far better than merely discussing
the mistake.

As your judgment improves, you will come to recognize when it's appropriate to amend the "rules" of angle play. For example, you should not come
as far off your line when the ball carrier has a teammate in a better shooting
position. You will also learn to read the ball carrier (for example, a player with
his eyes on the ball is unlikely to pass).

A Note to Coaches

At this point I'd like to interject some thoughts to you coaches who are working
with preteen goalies. It's a very rare youngster who is ready, either physically
or psychologically, to handle the demands of goalkeeping. As such, it's best to
rotate your players, having a number of them try their hands in goal.

If you do have some individuals who aspire to become keepers, do not push
them. Merely show them how to catch a ball correctly, let them field some
shots, and teach them how to cut down a shooter's angle.

One exercise that I recommend to develop hand–eye coordination is to
have the goalie lie flat on his back. From that position he must throw the ball
in the air with both hands and make the catch.

Unlike his older counterpart, the young goalie should only be segregated
from the rest of the squad for, at most, a fraction of the training session. Let
him learn the whole game and develop the skills of an outfield player.

For those who are mature enough to handle the position's demands, some helpful drills follow.

UP-AND-BACK DRILL

Goalkeepers must practice proper footwork, both when advancing and backpedaling. A good exercise to improve footwork begins with your heels on the goal line. Your server stands 25 to 30 yards upfield and slowly rolls a ball that you must sprint forward to collect. As soon as the play is made and the ball returned, the server lofts a shot at the goal. You must backpedal and either make the save cleanly or tip the ball over the crossbar. Under no circumstance should you turn your body; you must remain square to the shooter at all times.

ABOUT-FACE DRILL

Stand on your line while facing the net. On command, pivot to face the field of play just as your server takes a shot from 10 to 15 yards out. This drill helps to sharpen reflexes.

Diving over a willing teammate aids technique and forces the legs to achieve full thrust.

DIVING-OVER DRILL

An excellent drill to teach proper diving technique involves a server and a second teammate. The latter kneels on all fours, facing the server (who is 5 yards away). You stand to one side of your kneeling teammate. The server tosses the ball to the opposite side, forcing you to dive over the obstacle person to make the catch.

RUNNING A SIDELINE

You and the server stand 3 to 5 yards apart and begin running sideways in the same direction. The server tosses the ball in the direction in which both of you are moving. You must dive, make the save, return the ball to the server, and continue in the same direction. Continue this until you reach the midfield line, then change direction and repeat the drill to the goal line.

CATCHER'S SQUAT

Man your net with the server at the penalty spot. Start in a baseball catcher's squat. The server kicks shots that you can save, yet are reasonably challenging.

SOMERSAULT DRILLS

Stand next to one goalpost while facing the opposite post. The server is again positioned on the penalty spot. Somersault across the face of the goal. Just as you come to your feet, the server shoots the ball along the ground at the far post. You must dive to make the save *with two hands* before returning the ball to the server. Repeat the process in the opposite direction. Because this is a fatiguing exercise, limit repetitions to ten dives per set.

To learn to make point-blank reflex saves on rebounds, stand in the middle of your net on the line. The server should be stationed between the 6 yardline and the penalty spot, directly in front of you. Perform a forward roll. Just as you come to your feet, the server volleys the ball. You should be able to get to the ball, since it is kicked close to your body, even though the shot is struck with considerable pace. Don't worry about goalkeeping form on this type of save; concentrate, instead, on trying to prevent a score by using any and all parts of your body. If possible, deflect the rebound wide.

Goalkeeper's Somersault Drills

The side somersault drill aids agility, fitness, and concentration.

The forward roll, or "equilibrium drill,"
sharpens a goalie's rebounding reactions.

Sometimes a goalie must dive into a shooter's feet hoping the ball will strike him. To learn this blocking technique, roll the ball to a shooter, sprint forward, and dive across the plane of the goalmouth. You must dive early enough so that you are on the ground as the ball is kicked. Have the server always shoot the ball on the first touch.

One of the best is to have ten shooters (each with a ball) line up across the edge of the penalty area. The player to the far right takes a shot. You make the save and then move at full speed to face a shot from the player on the far left. The second shooter times his kick so that you must rush to make the play, yet reach the proper position as the ball is struck. This continues until all attackers have shot.

Another exercise to improve on-the-line technique is to have a server take several shots from varying distances. Sometimes the server may be your coach. Although his shooting technique may not be exceptional, he must refrain from throwing the ball because it is important that you get in the habit of looking

DIVING INTO FEET

An unpleasant, but necessary, part of goalkeeping is learning how to dive into a shooter's feet. Here, you turn yourself into as big a target as possible, hoping the ball will hit you.

One way to master this type of save is to face breakaways in practice. Another approach is a drill that begins with you on your line with the ball. Roll the ball to a shooter who is just outside of the penalty area. Then you must sprint toward the shooter and dive into his feet to make the save. Your coach should be certain that your body hits the ground at or before the instant the shooter receives the ball. Your hands should be outstretched, and the middle of your chest should bisect an imaginary line formed by the ball and the center of the goal.

FACING SHOTS

Only after your technique is relatively polished should you face shots. Making saves prior to that point will develop hard-to-break bad habits. Once you are ready, there are a number of good shooting drills.

downward at the shooter's feet at the time of the shot. In addition, the pace and angle of a kicked ball is markedly different from one that is thrown.

You'll also benefit greatly from participating in small-sided drills in which finishing is included.

BLINDFOLDED KEEPERS

The most unusual drill I've yet come across was described to me by 1981 NCAA Division I Coach of the Year Schellas Hyndman. Believe it or not, Hyndman blindfolds his goalies, who must react by *hearing* shots (which are taken along the ground).

The objective is to get all of a goalie's senses to concentrate on the ball. Making the save is not important; learning to dive in the right direction is all that matters.

Before you laugh at this unusual practice, you should note that Schellas first learned it when he trained with Brazil's famed São Paulo FC in 1976. At first, Schellas was skeptical of the drill's value. But when he saw its results and thought of how many times a keeper's sight is obstructed during goalmouth scrambles, he decided to give it a try at Eastern Illinois University. After all, he reasoned, a drill that's good enough for one of the world's premier professional teams might just be up to our standards, no matter how bizarre it sounds.

FITNESS

Although keepers do not need to attain the same stamina level required of outfield players, your fitness is still important. It is an accepted adage that a goalie is only as good as his legs. Your acceleration, leaping ability, and quickness can always be improved.

Repeated jumps over a ball improve leg strength.

There are many good exercises you can perform on your own, such as jumping over a stationary object, like a ball. Leap in sets of twenty-five or fifty, first jumping off of both feet, then with the outside foot (the foot away from the ball) and later off of the inside foot.

Another jumping drill involves a wall or the goalpost. Hold the ball over your head and leap, touching the ball against the object. Do this exercise in sets of twenty-five to fifty repetitions.

Although as a goalie you do only a modest amount of running during a game, you should nevertheless do short sprints and backpedaling.

Perhaps the best way to improve your legs is to dive off a soft surface. The Poles train their keepers on sand. This forces them to use extra power to obtain distance on their dives and is great for strengthening the legs. If there isn't a beach nearby, a sandpit can be constructed. Using sand aids diving in much the same way that a baseball hitter's bat speed improves from using a weighted bat in the on-deck circle. Not only will your legs benefit but the risk of injury is minimal, thanks to the soft surface.

Those of you who prefer the unorthodox can follow the example of Canadian National Team goalkeeper Tony Chursky. The NASL veteran credits ballet with providing much of his agility.

PRACTICING TEAM DEFENSE

Goalkeepers and their teams need to practice defending against set pieces, particularly corner kicks and free kicks in and around the penalty area.

You can practice corners through repetition. If you find yourself reluctant to leave your line, a good drill is to have a server strike crosses into the box, in which there are three or four attackers and *only* you on defense. You are thus forced to make aggressive plays, getting to the ball before any opponents.

When facing free kicks, you and your defense must learn to set up rapidly. This is even more important when erecting a wall.

Place three balls at various spots just outside the penalty box, with two attackers near each ball. Another six offensive players should position themselves off the ball, just as they would on a free kick. Your coach points to one of the three balls and you and your defense have 10 seconds (or less) to set up against a free kick from that spot.

On all set pieces you, as keeper, are in total control of your penalty area. You are the "coach on the field." Assertiveness, like diving technique, does not come naturally to most young goalies. You must *make* yourself assertive. The keeper who does not take charge of a game is not fulfilling his responsibilities.

CONFIDENCE

There is no other position in sport in which confidence is as fragile a commodity as it is for the soccer goalkeeper. A goalie whose self-belief is shattered will not take charge (he'll react instead of act) and is liable to make damaging errors.

You coaches out there: It is very important that you always—*always*—communicate with your goalie in a constructive manner and that you never—*never*—hinder the keeper's confidence. Removing a goalie from a match after he concedes a bad goal and yelling at him for a mistake are surefire ways of ruining his morale. Even great keepers, from Gordon Banks to Jan van Beveren, have yielded "soft" scores. When that happens to a goalie he must put it out of his mind, project a positive approach, and concern himself only with making the next play. And the coach and the goalie's teammates must be there to let him know they support him.

Coaching Priorities

Coaching soccer, particularly at the youth level, requires more than just a passing knowledge of the sport's basic skills. It is a responsibility: the type that comes with influencing and molding young minds. The priorities and attitudes expressed by the coach affect far more than just the outcome of a game.

That's why I'm particularly fond of the approach taken by such organizations as the YMCA and the AYSO. Their leadership has helped those involved in soccer do a commendable job in averting the well-documented abuses that have appeared in so many other team sports. Perhaps, too, the fact that the parent/spectator isn't as well versed in the game's rules as is his baseball or football counterpart has kept the sport clean and enjoyable.

Some individuals, however, have become "overenthusiastic." Regrettably, I have witnessed adults yelling at a hurt ten-year-old to stop "faking" an injury. I've also observed much uncalled-for complaining aimed at referees. When an adult acts in such a manner, he sets a horrible example for his child. Those who get "carried away" should receive a polite reminder from the youth coach about appropriate behavior.

181

Good coaches teach soccer *and* influence young minds in a positive fashion.

Good soccer parents are supportive,
encouraging, and enthusiastic.

The questions I'm most often asked by inexperienced coaches are "What formation is best for my youth team?" and "How can I decide which children are best suited for which position?" The answers that I usually give to these inquiries are "None" and "You can't."

Regarding formations, I feel it's best for younger players to engage in what the Canadian Soccer Association calls "Mini Soccer." Although CSA guidelines vary with each age group, the concept is to have subteenage players involved in small-sided matches on scaled-down fields with smaller goals and balls. Extensive studies have shown that eleven-a-side games on adult-sized fields with an adult-sized ball can frustrate the younger player. With twenty-one other players, a huge field, and only one ball, he doesn't feel like he's a part of the action a good deal of the time. Mini Soccer eliminates this problem.

Concerning leagues that insist on eleven-a-side games for young players: The less structured those games are, the better. Children are not usually attuned to positioning anyway. To force defenders to play only defense, especially when their team is on the attack, only frustrates kids. Sure, if you're a coach, you can assign individuals to play specific positions, but don't become upset when you find a youngster caught out of position.

As to how to allocate players, I feel that until a child reaches his middle teenage years, he shouldn't be labeled a "goalkeeper," "midfielder," "striker," etc. The great Dutch star Johan Cruyff credits his all-around abilities and his superb reading of the game to having played every position as a youngster.

Many proud parents point to their eight-year-old and assert, "He's going to be a great forward." They get angry at the coach who uses their child in any other position. What an ill-advised attitude! The eight-year-old who may be perfectly suited to play up front might develop into an outstanding midfielder if given the chance. No matter what position he ends up playing, he'll perform better if he's first experienced every situation and position during his formative years.

Simple as it may sound, the most important attribute you as a youth coach can bring to your team is the ability to keep soccer fun. Only one youngster in thousands will turn pro. That being the case, you should try to gear games and practices toward your team's improvement and enjoyment.

Basic skills and techniques need not be taught in a boot-camp atmosphere; they can be imparted in a manner that is challenging and stimulating. For example, turning the cone-dribbling drill into a competitive contest will help immeasurably toward this end.

As a coach, you will find that most youngsters tend to move faster than their skill level allows. Often, children participating in the cone drill will move so quickly that they lose control of the ball. Always remind players that pace is secondary—achieving good ball control by using proper technique is the top priority. Ironically, one of the best ways to impart this message is to make the cone drill into a relay race. The youngster who moves too fast will spend twice the time in retrieving the ball than if he'd taken his time.

Professional players, such as former Chicago Sting defender Greg Ryan, are often available for soccer clinics.

184   You must know your players' capabilities and limitations and design your practice accordingly. Do not ask youngsters to run before they can walk! Also, younger players' attention spans are short, so vary your training sessions, keep things moving, and keep drills interesting.

Not until players have reached high-school age should they be introduced to tactics or formations. Until that stage, you are better advised simply to teach the various skills of the game while maintaining an enjoyable atmosphere. A practice should never be boring, *even on the collegiate or professional level.*

Having read this book, I hope you now have a better understanding of soccer's basics. Nevertheless, you should consider this as nothing more than your first step toward becoming a knowledgeable soccer aficionado.

No written word can substitute for actually seeing how soccer skills are executed and trying them yourself. There are many great avenues open to you youth coaches and players if you seek them out. All NASL, MISL, and American Soccer League teams have active clinic programs. In addition, many major college teams will make guest appearances, upon request.

Both the CSA and USYSA (and their affiliated provincial or state associations) run coaching courses, as do many nonaffiliated groups (like the AYSO). There are scores of fine instructional soccer films that may be borrowed for a small fee or none at all.

In addition, I encourage parents and coaches to enroll in a first-aid course.

Knowledge of basic first-aid is a must if you're going to coach soccer.

With players like these leading the way, the rest of the world's most popular game may soon be North America's, too.

Although the injury factor fortunately is minimal in soccer, especially among young players, an adult at the field should know how to deal with medical problems that can arise.

Watching as many top college and/or professional games as possible is also a good idea. By *seeing* how first-quality athletes perform in a match, you gain a clearer notion of how soccer is meant to be played. This can be of particular help to you young players. By isolating your attention on a pro or college athlete who is performing at your favorite position, you can learn volumes about the game.

The great thing about soccer is that it offers benefits extending well beyond the game itself. The opportunity to travel and meet peers from around the world can have a profound effect on players of any age. To find out how to enter or to host such events, contact your national governing body. Both the CSA and USYSA's phone numbers are listed in the back of this book. Each organization also runs national championships for boys, girls, men, and women in several age categories that are open to all affiliated teams.

One final note: Parents who first become involved in soccer through their children need not limit their activities to volunteering to coach or officiate. Many adults have discovered that soccer is a great game to play. Even if your top competitive days are ancient history, you can still play this game. Run a bit less, have a substitute hold the fort for a few minutes while you catch your breath, and return for more fun.

I hope this book has proven to be a helpful guide and that you, as I have done, come to discover the great joy and personal growth that soccer offers to us all.

Glossary

Advantage Law: Rule that allows play to continue after a foul, if stopping the action would prove disadvantageous to the team that was fouled.

ASL: American Soccer League. The oldest professional league in the United States.

AYSO: American Youth Soccer Organization.

Ball carrier: The player in possession of the ball.

Ball-watching: Common mistake in which a defender is so intent on watching the ball that he isn't aware of the movement of the opponent he is assigned to mark.

Basket-hanging: Basketball term referring to a player who stations himself around the opposition net even when the ball is far away.

Bicycle Kick: Spectacular overhead kick.

Booking: A system whereby the referee writes down the name of a player who is being warned that any further misconduct will result in his ejection.

Bundesliga: West German First Division.

Cap: Appearance by a player for his National Team in an official international competition (such as the World Cup or World Cup qualifying matches).

Caution: Issuance of a yellow card.

Center: To pass the ball from near the sideline into the middle of the field, usually the penalty area.

Center forward: Once-common term that refers to the player whose main responsibility is scoring goals (also known as the striker).

Central defender: Defender who guards the middle of the field in front of his team's goal.

Charging: Illegally making body contact to knock an opponent off the ball.

Checking off: Off-the-ball movement by an attacker in which he runs away from the ball carrier to create space before turning into that space and running toward the ball.

Copa Libertadores: Annual tournament pitting championship professional teams from each South American nation.

Corner kick: Method of restarting play after the defending team has cleared the ball over the goal line. The ball is placed at the point where the sideline and goal line intersect, with the attacking team awarded a free kick that may be shot directly into the goal.

Counterattack: Offensive foray made by a team as soon as it has won possession of the ball.

Crisscross run: Off-the-ball movement in which two attackers' paths cross.

Cross: Same as a center.

CSA: Canadian Soccer Association. An affiliate of FIFA, it promotes and administers the sport in Canada.

Dangerous play: An action by a player that jeopardizes his or another player's safety. It is punished by an indirect free kick.

Defender: Player whose primary responsibility is to prevent the opposition from creating scoring opportunities.

Defensive midfielder: Player whose main job is to guard the opponents' most dangerous midfielder.

Diagonal run: Off-the-ball movement in which a player runs at an angle toward the opponents' goal line.

Direct free kick: A free kick in which a goal can be scored by kicking the ball straight into the opponent's net.

Direct kick offense: One of soccer's "major" fouls that results in a direct free kick being awarded.

Distribution: Pass made by the goalkeeper.

Dribbling: Act of advancing the ball with one's feet.

Dummy: Intentionally allowing the ball to roll through one's legs to a teammate after having pretended to kick the ball.

European Cup: Annual championship competition featuring championship professional teams from each European nation.

FA: Football Association (popular term for most nations' governing body, such as the "Scottish FA").

FA Cup: Annual single-elimination tournament open to all teams, both amateur and professional, in England.

Far post: The goalpost that is farthest from the ball.

FIFA: Federation Internationale de Football Association. The official governing body of soccer, it runs world championships, sets rules, and settles disputes between nations. The USSF and CSA are both members of FIFA.

FIFA World Youth Championship: Tournament held every odd year and open to every affiliated country's National Youth Team.

Finish: Shot.

Football: Worldwide term for soccer.

Footballer: Soccer player.

Formation: The numerical equation that describes how a team allocates its players.

Forward: An attacking player who is positioned close to the opposition goal.

4-4-2: Formation featuring four defenders, four midfielders, and twin strikers (forwards).

4-3-3: Popular formation featuring four defenders, three midfielders, and three forwards.

4-2-4: Formation featuring four defenders, two midfielders, and two forwards.

Friendly: Exhibition game.

Fullback: The defender who is positioned closest to the sideline.

Goalkeeper: The only player legally permitted to use his hands. It is his responsibility to prevent goals from being scored.

Goal kick: Method of restarting play when the attacking team last touched the ball before it crossed the goal line without entering the goal. The ball is placed 6 yards from the goal line with the defensive team awarded a free kick.

Goal line: The end boundary line running parallel to the goal.

Goalmouth: Area in front of the goal.

Halfback: Midfielder.

Half-volley: Kicking the ball on the first touch after it bounces.

Hand ball: Direct-free-kick offense that results when any outfield player intentionally touches the ball with his hand and/or arm.

Hat trick: Scoring of three or more goals by a single player in one game.

Heading: Act of redirecting the ball with one's head.

Indirect free kick: A free kick in which the ball must touch at least two players before a goal can be scored.

Indirect-free-kick offense: A foul that results in an indirect free kick being awarded.

Injury time: Time added to a period to compensate for stoppages due to injuries, the scoring of a goal, or time-wasting.

Inside foot: The foot closer to the opponent or the goal.

Interchanging run: Same as a crisscross run.

Into touch: Crossing from the playing field over the sideline. (Such as, "The ball rolled into touch.")

Juggling: Practice exercise in which a player prevents the ball from touching the ground without using his hands or arms.

Keepaway: Act of maintaining possession while preventing the opponent(s) from getting the ball.

Kick-and-run soccer: Style of play in which a team boots the ball aimlessly upfield and then chases after it.

Killer pass: A service that sets a teammate up for a good scoring opportunity.

Kit: Soccer uniform.

Libero: Sweeper.

Linesman: One of two officials whose job is to aid the referee.

Linkman: Term used to refer to the midfielder(s) whose job is to provide a bridge between his team's defenders and forwards.

Lob: Lofted kick.

Maestro: The midfielder who orchestrates his team's attack.

Manager: Coach.

Marking: Act of guarding an opponent.

Midfielder: Player who provides a link between his team's forwards and defenders.

MISL: Major Indoor Soccer League.

NASL: North American Soccer League.

National Amateur Team: An all-star collection of a nation's best amateur players representing their country in international competition, such as the Olympic Games.

National Team: An all-star collection of players, nearly always professionals, who represent their country in international competition, such as the World Cup.

National Youth Team: An all-star collection of players under 19 who represent their country in international competition, such as the FIFA Youth World Championship for the Coca-Cola Cup.

NCAA: National Collegiate Athletic Association, the major governing body of college soccer in the U.S.

Near post: The goalpost closer to the ball.

Nutmeg: Advancing past an opponent by kicking the ball through his legs.

Obstruction: Illegally preventing an opponent from playing the ball by blocking his path to the ball.

Offside: Infraction in which an offensive player does not have at least two defensive players between himself and the goal line when the ball is played forward by a member of the attacking team.

Off-the-ball movement: Movement by attacking players not in possession that is used to get open or to create space for a teammate.

Outfield player: Any player other than the goalkeeper.

Overlapping: Attacking foray by a defender with the ball, in which he advances past the midfield area.

Over the Top: Especially vicious foul in which the tackler's foot goes over the ball and his cleats strike the ball carrier's leg.

Own goal: A goal scored for the opposition by inadvertently deflecting the ball into the goal one is defending.

Penalty arc: Semicircle at the top of the penalty area into which no player may encroach as a penalty kick is shot.

Penalty area: The 44-by-18-yard zone in front of each goal.

Penalty kick: Direct free kick from 12 yards in front of the net involving a one-on-one confrontation between the shooter and the goalkeeper. It results when a team commits one of soccer's "major" fouls within its own penalty area.

Penalty spot: Place from where a penalty kick is taken.

Penetrating pass: A downfield pass that goes past one or more defensive players before reaching the receiver.

Pitch: Field.

Point of attack: Angle from which the ball carrier is moving toward the defense.

Professional foul: Intentional foul used to gain a tactical advantage. It is usually committed by a defensive player against the ball carrier just outside of the penalty area.

Promotion/relegation system: System used in many countries in which a specific number of teams finishing at the bottom of the first division are demoted to the second division for the following season while an equal number of clubs who finished at the top of the second division are promoted to next year's first division. (Note: In England there are four divisions with three teams promoted to the first, second, and third divisions every year and three teams relegated to the second, third, and fourth divisions annually.)

Pushing: Illegally using one's arms or hands against an opponent.

Push pass: Pass made with the inside of the foot, usually over a short distance.

Red card: Card that is held aloft by the referee to signify that a player is being ejected from the match.

Referee: Official who has exclusive decision-making power.

Reserve team: Players on a professional team who are not first-team starters. They usually take part in matches against other reserve teams to hone their skills and fitness.

Save: Act by the goalkeeper made to prevent a score by catching or deflecting the ball.

SC: Soccer Club.

Scissors kick: Same as a bicycle kick.

Service: Pass.

Shielding: Art of maintaining possession by legally using one's body so that the defender is unable to touch the ball without fouling.

Shoot-out: Tie-breaking procedure introduced by the NASL in which players try to beat the opposing goalie on a breakaway within a 5-second period.

Sideline: Border of the playing field that runs perpendicular to the goal line.

Sliding tackle: Dispossessing the ball carrier by sliding along the ground to kick the ball away.

Small-sided game: A game involving considerably fewer than eleven players per team on a field that is smaller than regulation size.

Square ball: Pass that travels parallel to the goal line.

Stopper: Defender who must mark the opponents' most dangerous player, usually the striker.

Striker: Forward whose primary responsibility is to score goals.

Strong side: Part of the field to the side of the goal that is closer to the ball.

Strong-side attacker/defender: Attacker or defender who is on the strong side.

Sudden death: Tie-breaking procedure in which the game ends as soon as one team scores.

Supporting: Player off the ball moving to aid a teammate who is in possession (offensive supporting) or marking the ball carrier (defensive supporting).

Sweeper: Extra defender with no specific opponent to guard. He picks up the first unmarked opponent to enter into a dangerous attacking position or moves to gain possession of stray balls.

Tackling: Defensive skill of legally dispossessing the ball carrier.

3–4–3: Formation featuring three defenders, four midfielders, and three forwards.

3–3–4: Formation featuring three defenders, three midfielders, and four forwards.

Through ball: A pass struck behind the defense and into space for the intended receiver to run onto.

Throw-in: Method of restarting play when the ball crosses the sideline, in which a player tosses the ball by using both hands in an overhead motion while keeping both feet on the ground.

Total soccer: Tactical approach to soccer in which all of a team's players attack when their side has the ball and all defend when without it.

Touch: Making contact with the ball.

Touchline: Sideline.

Trapping: Bringing the ball under control through use of any part of the body except the hands or arms.

USSF: United States Soccer Federation. An affiliate of FIFA, it is the official governing body of the sport in the United States.

USYSA: United States Youth Soccer Association. The branch of the USSF that oversees all matters pertaining to players age 19 and under in the U.S.

Volley: Act of kicking a ball in midair.

Wall: Human blockage of players used to defend against a free kick.

Wall pass: A first-touch return pass made back to the original ball carrier.

Weak side: Part of the field to the side of the goal farther from the ball.

Weak-side attacker/defender: An attacker or defender who is on the weak side.

Wingback: Fullback.

Winger: Widest forward, whose primary responsibility is to set up teammates for scoring opportunities.

Winghalf: Widest midfielder.

Withdrawn player: An attacker who is behind the ball, usually used to refer to a midfielder or a defender.

World Cup: Championship competition held every four years that is open to the National Team of every country that is a member of FIFA.

W-M: Once-popular formation featuring three defenders, two halfbacks, and five forwards.

YMCA: Young Men's Christian Association.

Yellow card: Card held aloft by the referee that serves as an official warning to a player that any further misconduct will result in that player being ejected from the match.

Resources

AMERICAN SOCCER LEAGUE
532 Main Street
Bethlehem, PA 18018
(215) 868-2213

CANADIAN SOCCER ASSOCIATION
333 River Road
Ottawa, ON K1L8B9
(Youth Coordinator—Chris Bellamy)
(613) 746-1460

MAJOR INDOOR SOCCER LEAGUE
1 Bala Plaza
Bala Cynwyd, PA 19004
(215) 667-8020

NORTH AMERICAN
SOCCER LEAGUE
1133 Avenue of the Americas
New York, NY 10036
(Youth Coordinator—
Howie Charbonneau)
(212) 575-0066

UNITED STATES SOCCER
FEDERATION
Youth Administrator Office
350 Fifth Avenue
Suite 4010
New York, NY 10118
(212) 736-0915